W9-ACK-184

SCOTT FORESMAN · ADDISON WESLEY

Mathematics

Grade 4

Every Student Learns

With a Foreword by Dr. Jim Cummins

ESL Consultant
Darrel Nickolaisen
Teacher/Consultant
Apple Valley, California

PEARSON
Scott Foresman

Editorial Offices: Glenview, Illinois • Parsippany, New Jersey • New York, New York

Sales Offices: Parsippany, New Jersey • Duluth, Georgia • Glenview, Illinois
Coppell, Texas • Ontario, California • Mesa, Arizona

Overview

Every Student Learns is a lesson-by-lesson companion to
Scott Foresman - Addison Wesley Mathematics and Matemáticas Scott
Foresman - Addison Wesley. It has been designed to provide manageable
support for teachers and their students who are challenged by language issues in
Mathematics, no matter what the first language may be.

Every Student Learns is built upon the Three Pillars of English Language Learning
in the Content Areas by Dr. Jim Cummins of the University of Toronto:

• Activate Prior Knowledge/Build Background

• Access Content

• Extend Language

ISBN: 0-328-07553-1

All Rights Reserved. Printed in the United States of America. This publication
is protected by Copyright, and permission should be obtained from the publisher
prior to any prohibited reproduction, storage in a retrieval system, or transmission
in any form by any means, electronic, mechanical, photocopying, recording, or
likewise. For information regarding permission(s), write to: Permissions
Department, Scott Foresman, 1900 East Lake Avenue, Glenview, Illinois 60025.

7 8 9 10 V004 09 08 07 06

Table of Contents

Supporting ESL Students
in Learning the Language of Mathematics

DR. JIM CUMMINS • UNIVERSITY OF TORONTO

Mathematics and Language

Mathematics can legitimately be considered to be a language in itself in that it employs symbols to represent concepts, symbols that facilitate our thinking about aspects of reality. However, mathematics is also intimately related to the natural language that we begin to acquire as infants, the language we use to communicate in a variety of everyday and academic contexts. Mathematics and language are interconnected at several levels:

- Teachers use natural language to explain mathematical concepts and perform mathematical operations. Students who have limited proficiency in English require additional support in order to understand mathematical concepts and operations taught in English. Among the supports that teachers can use to make instruction comprehensible for English language learners are demonstrations; concrete, hands-on manipulatives and graphic organizers; simplification and paraphrasing of instructional language; and direct teaching of key vocabulary.

- As is the case in other academic disciplines, mathematics uses a specialized technical vocabulary to represent concepts and, in the case of mathematics, describe operations. As early as Grade 1, students are required to learn the meanings of such words as *addition, subtraction, sum,* and *addend,* words that are likely to be found only in mathematics discourse. Furthermore, other terms have specific meanings in mathematics discourse that differ from their meanings in everyday usage and in other subject areas. Examples of these kinds of terms include words such as *table, product, even,* and *odd.* Homophones such as *sum* and *some* may also be confusing for ESL students. Grade 1 students are required to learn key concepts, such as *number facts* and *addition sentences,* at a time when many of them (ESL students, in particular) may not know the broader meanings of words such as *facts* and *sentences.*

- In addition to the technical vocabulary of mathematics, language intersects with mathematics at the broader level of general vocabulary, syntax, semantics, and discourse. Most mathematical problems require students to understand propositions and logical relations that are expressed through language. Consider this problem at the Grade 4 level:

    Wendy gave a total of 10 treats to her dogs. She gave her large dog 2 more treats than she gave her small dog. How many treats did she give to each dog?

Here students need to understand (or be able to figure out) the meanings of words such as *total* and *treats.* They need to understand the logical relation expressed by the *more ... than ...* construction. And they need to infer that Wendy has only two dogs, even though this fact is not explicitly included in the problem. Clearly, the language demands of the math curriculum increase as students progress through the grades, and these demands can cause particular difficulties for ESL students.

© Pearson Education, Inc., 4

The ESL Challenge

Numerous research studies have demonstrated that ESL students generally require at least 5 years to catch up to native speakers in academic language proficiency (i.e., reading and writing skills; see Cummins, 2001 for a review). In mathematics, ESL students often make good progress in acquiring basic computation skills in the early grades. However, they typically experience greater difficulty in learning to interpret and solve word problems, and this difficulty increases in the later elementary grades as the word problems become more linguistically and conceptually complex.

These developmental patterns can be understood in relation to three very different aspects of language proficiency:

- **Conversational fluency** is the ability to carry on a conversation in familiar face-to-face situations. This is the kind of proficiency that the vast majority of native speakers of English have developed by the time they enter school at age 5. It involves the use of high-frequency words and simple grammatical constructions. ESL students generally develop basic fluency in conversational aspects of English within a year or two of exposure to the language, either within school or in their out-of-school environments.

- **Discrete language skills** reflect specific phonological, lexical, and grammatical knowledge that students can acquire in two ways: (a) as a result of direct instruction and (b) through both formal and informal practice (e.g., reading). Some of these discrete language skills are acquired early in schooling, and some continue to be acquired throughout schooling. The discrete language skills that are acquired early include knowledge of the letters of the alphabet, the sounds represented by individual letters and combinations of letters, and the ability to decode written words and pronounce them appropriately. ESL students can learn these specific language skills at a relatively early stage in their acquisition of English; in fact, these skills can be learned concurrently with their development of basic vocabulary and conversational proficiency.

  In mathematics, these discrete language skills include knowledge of the symbols that represent basic mathematical operations (e.g., + and −), the terms used to refer to these symbols and operations (*add, subtract, plus, minus,* etc.), and the basic technical vocabulary of mathematics. Clearly, the ability to decode written text is also a necessary (but not a sufficient) condition for thinking through and solving word problems expressed in written language.

- **Academic language proficiency** includes knowledge of the less frequent vocabulary of English as well as the ability to interpret and produce increasingly complex written language. As students progress through the grades, they encounter far more low-frequency words (primarily from Greek and Latin sources), complex syntax (e.g., the passive voice), and abstract expressions that are virtually never heard in everyday conversation. Students are required to understand linguistically and conceptually demanding texts in the content areas (e.g., literature, social studies, science, and mathematics) and to use this increasingly sophisticated language in accurate and coherent ways in their own writing.

© Pearson Education, Inc., 4

Acquiring academic language proficiency is challenging for all students. Schools spend at least 12 years trying to extend the conversational language that native-speaking children bring to school into these more complex academic language spheres. It is hardly surprising, therefore, that research has repeatedly shown that ESL students usually require at least 5 years of exposure to academic English in order to catch up to native-speaker norms. In addition to internalizing increasingly complex academic language, ESL students must catch up to a moving target. Every year, native speakers are making large gains in their reading and writing abilities and in their knowledge of vocabulary. In order to catch up to grade norms within 6 years, ESL students must make 15 months' gain in every 10-month school year. By contrast, the typical native-speaking student is expected to make 10 months' gain in a 10-month school year (Collier & Thomas, 1999).

All three aspects of language proficiency are important. However, the three aspects—conversational fluency, discrete language skills, and academic language proficiency—are frequently confused by policy makers and by the media. For example, it is sometimes claimed that children acquire language rapidly and that one year of instructional support is sufficient to enable ESL students to catch up academically. In reality, many ESL students who have acquired fluent conversational skills are still a long way from grade-level performance in academic language proficiency (e.g., in reading comprehension in content areas such as math).

Similarly, the learning of discrete language skills does not generalize automatically to academic language proficiency. ESL (and native-speaking) students who can "read" a mathematical problem fluently may have only a very limited understanding of the words and sentences they can decode.

Thus, ESL students may require extended language support within the classroom in order to continue to make grade-level progress in content areas such as mathematics. Despite the fact that these students have acquired conversational fluency in English, together with basic mathematical vocabulary and computational skills, they may still experience gaps in their knowledge of some of the more sophisticated vocabulary, syntax, and discursive features of mathematical language.

Teaching the Language of Mathematics

From an instructional perspective, the relationship between language and mathematics is both two-way and reciprocal. Mathematical knowledge is developed through language, and language abilities can and should be developed through mathematics instruction. Specifically:

- Because mathematical concepts and operations are embedded in language, the specialized vocabulary of mathematics and the discursive features of mathematical propositions must be taught explicitly if students are to make strong academic progress in mathematics.

- Equally important, however, is the fact that in teaching mathematics, we are also developing and reinforcing students' general academic language proficiency. For example, think about the language learning that will likely occur as the teacher explains the following Grade 1 problem to a group of ESL students.

   Is 3 + 8 greater than 10, equal to 10, or less than 10? Explain.

© Pearson Education, Inc., 4

Students will learn not only the specific meanings of the terms *greater than, equal to,* and *less than,* but also synonyms for these terms (e.g., a synonym for *great* is *big,* and the meaning of *greater than* is similar to the meaning of *bigger than*). This particular mathematics problem also presents the teacher an opportunity to teach students the general concept of *comparatives* and the general rule for forming comparatives (e.g., *great, greater, greatest; big, bigger, biggest*). The fact that not all comparatives take exactly these forms can also be taught in relation to *less, lesser, least.* Finally, the meaning of the word explain can be taught (e.g., *describe, tell about, tell why you think so*) and related to its use in other subject areas (e.g., science).

The reciprocal interdependence of language and mathematics becomes apparent, and even obvious, when perusing any mathematics textbook. Much of what students are expected to learn in mathematics is presented in written text. Students are required to read the text in order to develop their understanding of math concepts and their ability to solve math problems. Frequently, students are also required to explain orally or in writing how they solved a particular problem. Obviously, teachers and students will discuss these concepts; but without strong reading skills, students will find it very difficult to acquire, and truly assimilate, lesson content. Without strong writing skills, they will have difficulty demonstrating their knowledge of the concepts and skills that they are often, in fact, acquiring. Thus, effective reading and writing skills are necessary for students to make progress in mathematics, particularly as they move through the elementary grades. By the same token, the teaching of mathematics provides important opportunities for teachers to model academic language in their interactions with students and also to teach features of academic language directly (e.g., reading comprehension strategies, comparative adjectives, and context- or content-specific vocabulary).

Effective academic language instruction for ESL students across the curriculum is built on three fundamental pillars:

- **Activate Prior Knowledge/Build Background**
- **Access Content**
- **Extend Language**

In developing mathematical knowledge through language, and language abilities through mathematics, we can apply these three instructional principles in powerful ways.

Activate Prior Knowledge/Build Background

A. Prior knowledge as the foundation of learning

There is general agreement among cognitive psychologists that we learn by integrating new input into our existing cognitive structures or schemata. Our prior experience provides the foundation for interpreting new information. No learner is a blank slate. In fact, learning can be defined as the process of relating new information to the information we already possess. When we read a mathematical problem, for example, we construct meaning by bringing our prior knowledge of language, of mathematics, and of the world in general to the text. Our prior knowledge enables us to make inferences about the meanings of words and expressions that we may not have encountered before. As our prior knowledge expands through new learning, we are enabled to understand a greater range of mathematical concepts and also the language that expresses those concepts.

© Pearson Education, Inc., 4

Thus, a major rationale for activating students' prior knowledge (or if there is minimal prior knowledge on a particular topic or issue, building it with students), is to make the learning process more efficient. It is important to *activate* students' prior knowledge because students may not explicitly realize what they know about a particular topic or issue; consequently, their prior knowledge may not facilitate learning unless it is brought to an immediate, and conscious, level.

B. Prior knowledge and ESL students

In a classroom that includes second-language learners from diverse backgrounds, prior knowledge about a particular topic may vary widely. Thus, simple transmission of certain information or a given skill will fail to connect with the prior knowledge and previous experience of many students. As a result, the input will be much less comprehensible for these students. Some students may have relevant information in their first language (L1), but not realize that there is any connection with what they are learning in English (L2). In other cases, the algorithms and strategies that students have acquired for carrying out math operations in their countries of origin may differ considerably from the procedures they are now being taught in English. Clearly, these discrepancies can cause confusion for students.

In teaching math to ESL students, it is important that we attempt to connect the instruction both with students' prior experience of learning math and with their prior knowledge of the world in general. In building up our own knowledge of students' educational and cultural backgrounds, we can collaborate with ESL teachers, who may have greater access to this information, and also with community volunteers, who can often provide invaluable insights about students' prior learning and cultural knowledge.

Lois Meyer (2000) has expressed clearly the importance of prior knowledge (familiarity with a given topic) in reducing the cognitive load of instruction for ESL students. She notes that the notion of *cognitive load* refers to the number and complexity of new concepts embedded in a particular lesson or text. This cognitive load depends not only on the text itself but also on the students' prior knowledge of the content.

> If the English learner has little entry knowledge about the subject matter, the cognitive load of the lesson will be heavy, for many concepts will be new and unfamiliar. The student will have little basis from which to generate hypotheses regarding the meanings the teacher is conveying through English.

> If the student's entry knowledge of the topic is considerable, this will lighten the cognitive load. Learners can draw on their knowledge to interpret linguistic and non-linguistic clues in the lesson in order to make educated guesses about the meanings of the teacher's talk and text (2000, p. 229).

Clearly, the cognitive load of many mathematical texts is considerable, particularly as students progress through the grades. Finding out what students know about a particular topic allows the teacher to supply relevant concepts or vocabulary that some or all students may be lacking, but which will be important for understanding the upcoming text or lesson. Building this context permits students to understand more complex language and to pursue more cognitively demanding activities. It lessens the cognitive load of the text and frees up students' brain power.

© Pearson Education, Inc., 4

C. Strategies for Activating Prior Knowledge and Building Background

Three types of prior knowledge are relevant to consider in teaching mathematics: prior knowledge of math; knowledge that has been acquired through direct experiences; and knowledge acquired through secondary sources (e.g. books, videos, etc.). We can use brainstorming, role playing, and simulations, as well as connections to literature and other content areas to activate students' prior knowledge and build relevant background knowledge.

- **Connect to Prior Knowledge of Math** In Grade 1 we might activate students' knowledge of counting as a prelude to teaching them to use *counting on* as a tool for addition. Or at the Grade 4 level, we might activate students' knowledge of basic multiplication facts in order to reinforce the foundation for teaching more complex multiplication operations.

- **Connect to Prior Knowledge of Language** Although mathematics has its own technical language that students must learn, we explain this language, and the associated math operations, using more familiar everyday language. For example, in explaining the concept of *subtraction* we will use high frequency expressions such as *take away from* that are likely to be much more familiar to children. Typically, the meaning of this language will be reinforced through demonstrations involving concrete manipulatives or graphic organizers.

- **Connect to Prior Experiences** We can find out from students what activities they engage in outside of school and link mathematics instruction to those activities (e.g., students who engage in various sports can carry out a variety of operations relevant to those sports, such as calculating, comparing, and contrasting batting averages). We can also be proactive in *creating experiences* for students that will promote mathematical knowledge and skill. For example, we might engage parents as collaborators by having them work with their children in calculating the proportion of weekly food expenditures that the family spends on the various food groups, thereby reinforcing both social studies and math concepts.

- **Use Brainstorming, Role Playing, and Simulation** At a very early age most children develop an intuitive sense of "fairness" and an ability to judge whether goods of various kinds (e.g., toys or treats) have been distributed equally or fairly. We can use brainstorming, role-playing, and simulation to carry out a variety of math activities that tap into students' real-life experiences of equal (or fair) distribution. In the early grades, we would likely use concrete manipulatives to support these activities. In intermediate grades, real or simulated data can be used.

We can also link math to the development of critical thinking by having students carry out projects that go beyond the curriculum in various ways. For example, in a class with many ESL students we might have students brainstorm about the languages they know and how they learned them. On the basis of this brainstorming, they could then develop a questionnaire and carry out a more formal survey of the linguistic make-up of the class (or even the entire school). In analyzing data that reflect their own experiences and identities, students' motivation to explore effective analytic strategies and presentation tools (e.g., graphs and computerized slide shows) is likely to be considerably greater than when the activities are more distant from their experiences and interests.

© Pearson Education, Inc., 4

- **Use Literature and Connections to Content** Relatively few people in North America have ever been in a jungle, but most adults and children can describe the main features of jungles as a result of secondary experiences of various sorts. In the classroom, we can use literature, high-interest expository texts, and other forms of media (e.g., videotapes) both to activate students' prior knowledge of math and also to build background knowledge.

  In some cases, connecting to prior experiences will involve use of stories that have been specifically selected because they contain relevant math content. In other cases, we will connect math concepts and operations to other subject matter across the curriculum. For example, we might link math to a social studies unit on government as we discuss where local and state governments get the funds to operate and as we have students calculate the sales taxes that their families pay for various kinds of purchases.

The essential point here is that the more connections we can make both to students' experiences and interests and to other areas of the curriculum, the more relevance math is likely to assume in students' minds and lives. This, in turn, will result in more powerful learning of math.

An additional consideration in activating ESL Students' prior knowledge is that this process communicates a sense of respect for what students already know and an interest in their cultural backgrounds. This affirmation of students' identities increases students' personal and academic confidence and motivates them to invest their identities more strongly in pursuing academic success.

Access Content

How can teachers make the complex language of mathematics comprehensible for students who are still in the process of learning English? How can students be enabled to take ownership of their learning of math concepts and operations rather than just learn rote procedures? One important strategy has already been noted in the previous section. Activating and building students' background knowledge is an essential part of the process of helping students to participate academically and gain access to meaning. When we activate students' prior knowledge we attempt to modify the "soil" so that the seeds of meaning can take root. However, we can also support or *scaffold* students' learning by modifying the input itself. We provide this scaffolding by embedding the content in a *richly redundant context* wherein there are multiple routes to the mathematical meaning at hand in addition to the language itself.

The following list presents a variety of ways of modifying the presentation of mathematical content to ESL students so that they can more effectively get access to the meaning in any given lesson.

- **Use Demonstration** Teachers can take students through a word problem in math, demonstrating step-by-step procedures and strategies in a clear and explicit manner.

- **Use Manipulatives (and Tools and Technology)** In the early grades manipulatives may include counters and blocks that enable students to carry out a mathematical operation, literally with their hands, and actually see the concrete results of that operation. At more advanced levels, measuring tools such as rulers and protractors and technological

© Pearson Education, Inc., 4

aids such as calculators and computers will be used. The effectiveness of these tools will be enhanced if they are used within the context of a project that students are intrinsically motivated to initiate and complete.

- **Use Small-Group Interactions and Peer Questioning** Working either as a whole class or in heterogeneous groups or pairs, students can engage in real-life or simulated projects that require application of a variety of mathematical skills. Díaz-Rico and Weed (2002) give as an example a project in which students are told that the classroom needs to be re-carpeted. They first estimate the area and then check their estimates with measuring tools. Working in groups, students could also calculate the potential cost of floor coverings using prices for various types of floor coverings obtained from local catalogues or advertisements.

- **Use Pictures, Real Objects, and Graphic Organizers** We commonly hear the expression "A picture is worth a thousand words." There is a lot of truth to this when it comes to teaching academic content. Visuals enable students to "see" the basic concept we are trying to teach much more effectively than if we rely only on words. Once students grasp the concept, they are much more likely to be able to figure out the meanings of the words we use to talk about it. Among the visuals we can use in presenting math content are these: *pictures/photographs, real objects, graphic organizers, drawings on overhead projectors,* and *blackline masters.* Graphic organizers are particularly useful because they can be used not only by teachers to present concepts but also by students to take notes, organize their ideas in logical categories, and summarize the results of group brainstorming on particular issues. Some graphic organizers that are useful for teaching math are *Venn diagrams; pie and bar graphs; K-W-L charts* (What we know, what we want to know, and what we have learned; *T-charts* (e.g., for comparing and contrasting); *Problem and Solution charts; Main Idea and Details charts; Cause and Effect charts; Sequence charts;* and *Time Lines.*

- **Clarify Language (Paraphrase Ideas, Enunciate Clearly, Adjust Speech Rate, and Simplify Sentences)** This category includes a variety of strategies and language-oriented activities that clarify the meanings of new words and concepts. Teachers can modify their language to students by *paraphrasing ideas and by explaining new concepts and words.* They can explain new words by providing synonyms, antonyms, and definitions either in English or in the home language of students, if they know it. Important vocabulary can be repeated and recycled as part of the paraphrasing of ideas. Teachers should speak in a natural rhythm, but enunciate clearly and adjust their speech to a rate that ESL students will find easier to understand. Meaning can also be communicated and/or reinforced through gestures, body language, and demonstrations.

Because of their common roots in Latin and Greek, much of the technical math vocabulary in English has cognates in Romance languages, such as Spanish (e.g., *addition—adición*). Students who know these languages can be encouraged to make these cross-linguistic linkages as a means of reinforcing the concept. Bilingual and English-only dictionaries can also be useful tools for language clarification, particularly for intermediate-grade students.

© Pearson Education, Inc., 4

- **Use Total Physical Response, Gestures, and Pantomime** For beginning ESL Students, *Total Physical Response,* activities wherein students act out commands, can be highly effective. Math calculations can be embedded in the commands that students act out. For example, students can progress from fully acting out the command "Take 5 steps forward and then 2 steps backward" to calculating in their heads that they need take only 3 steps forward to reach the destination. Additionally, the meanings of individual words can be demonstrated through *gestures* and *pantomime.*

- **Give Frequent Feedback and Expand Student Responses** *Giving frequent feedback* means responding positively and naturally to all forms of responses. Teachers can let their students know how they are doing by responding to both their words and their actions. Teachers can also assess their students' understanding by asking them to give examples, or by asking them how they would explain a concept or idea to someone else. *Expanding student responses* often means using polar (either/or) questions with students who are just beginning to produce oral English and "wh" (who, what, when, where, why) questions with students who are more fluent. Teachers can easily, and casually, expand their students' one- and two-word answers into complete sentences ("Yes, a triangle does have three sides") and respond to grammatically incorrect answers by recasting them using standard English syntax (Student: "I gotted 4 tens and 1 one"; Teacher: "That's right, you have 4 tens and 1 one").

Extend Language

A systematic focus on and exploration of language is essential if students are to develop knowledge of the specific vocabulary and discursive patterns within the genre of mathematical language. As noted above, investigation of the language of mathematics can also develop in students a curiosity about language and deepen their understanding of how words work. Three strategies for extending students' knowledge of the language of mathematics are outlined below.

A. Creating mathematical language banks

Students can systematically collect the meanings of words and phrases they encounter in mathematical texts in a personal or group *language bank.* Ideally, the language bank would be created in a series of files within the classroom computer but it can also be done with paper and pencil in a class notebook.

Paradoxically, the complexity of mathematical language provides some important opportunities for language exploration. As mentioned above, a large percentage of the less frequent academic and technical vocabulary of English derives from Latin and Greek roots. One implication of this is that word formation follows some very predictable patterns. These patterns are similar in English and Spanish.

When students know some of the rules or conventions of how academic words are formed, it gives them an edge in extending their vocabulary. It helps them figure out not only the meanings of individual words but also how to form different parts of speech from those words.

© Pearson Education, Inc., 4

A central aspect of academic language is *nominalization.* This refers to the process whereby abstract nouns are formed from verbs and adjectives. Take, for example, four common verbs that occur in the math curriculum: *multiply, divide, measure,* and *equal.* The word families (excluding verb forms and plurals) for each of these words are presented below.

Verb	Noun	Adjective
multiply	multiplication multiple multiplicity	multiple
divide	division dividend	divisive divided
measure	measure measurement	measured
equal equalize	equality equal equalizer	equal equitable

We see in these four word families, several common ways in which the English language forms nouns from verbs. One pattern is to add the suffix *-tion* or *-ion* to the verb form as in *multiplication, division,* and many other mathematical terms, such as *estimation, notation,* and *operation.* Another pattern is to add the suffix *-ment* as in *measurement,* while a third pattern is to add the suffix *-ity* or *-ty* as in *equality, capacity, property,* and *probability.* When we demystify how this academic language works, students are more likely to recognize parts of speech in their reading of complex texts across the curriculum and to become more adept at inferring meaning from context. For example, when a student recognizes that *acceleration* is a noun (rather than a verb or an adjective), he or she is one step closer to understanding the meaning of the term in the context of a particular sentence or text.

Students can be encouraged to use dictionaries (in both English and their L1, when available) to explore the more subtle meanings of these mathematical words. For example, students could be asked to work in pairs or small groups to think through the differences in meaning between the verbs *equal* and *equalize;* among the nouns *equality, equal,* and *equalizer;* and between the adjectives *equal* and *equitable.*

© Pearson Education, Inc., 4

This nominalization process also permits us to think in terms of abstract realities or states and to use higher-level cognitive functions that require uses of language very different from the conversational or "playground" language that we acquire in everyday situations. This point is made clearly by Pauline Gibbons:

> The playground situation does not normally offer children the opportunity to use such language as: *if we increase the angle by 5 degrees, we could cut the circumference into equal parts.* Nor does it normally require the language associated with the higher-order thinking skills, such as hypothesizing, evaluating, inferring, generalizing, predicting, or classifying. Yet these are the language functions which are related to learning and the development of cognition; they occur in all areas of the curriculum, and without them a child's potential in academic areas cannot be realized (1991, p. 3).

Gibbons goes on to point out that explicit modeling of academic language is particularly important in schools with large numbers of ESL students:

> In such a school it is very easy to fall into the habit of constantly simplifying our language because we expect not to be understood. But if we only ever use basic language such as *put in* or *take out* or *go faster,* some children will not have any opportunity to learn other ways of expressing these ideas, such as *insert* or *remove* or *accelerate.* And these are the words that are needed to refer to the general concepts related to the ideas, such as *removal, insertion,* and *acceleration* (1991, p. 18).

In short, when students know some of the rules or conventions of how academic words are formed, it gives them an edge in extending their vocabulary. It helps them figure out not only the meanings of individual words but also how to form different parts of speech from these words. One way of organizing students' language detective work in mathematics is to focus separately on *meaning, form,* and *use.* Working in pairs or small groups, students can be encouraged to collect and explore one mathematics word per day, focusing on one or more of these three categories.

- **Focus on Meaning** Categories that can be explored within a Focus on Meaning include *Mathematical meaning; Everyday meaning; Meaning in other subject areas; L1 equivalents; Related words in L1 (cognates); Synonyms; Antonyms; Homonyms; Meaning of prefix; Meaning of root;* and *Meaning of suffix.* Not all of these categories will be relevant for every word, but considered together they provide a map of directions that an exploration of meaning might pursue. Take a possible exploration of the word *subtract:*

Mathematical meaning:	take one number or quantity from another (or compare two numbers or quantities)
L1 equivalent (Spanish):	restar, sustraer
Synonym:	deduct
Antonym:	add
Meaning of prefix:	under or away
Meaning of root:	from the Latin for "pull"

© Pearson Education, Inc., 4

• **Focus on Form** Most of the root words in mathematics that come from Latin and Greek form not just one part of speech; we can make nouns, verbs, and adjectives from many of these root words. If we know the typical patterns for forming nouns and adjectives from root verbs, we can recognize these parts of speech when they appear in text. The implications for expanding students' vocabulary are clear: rather than learning just one word in isolation, students are enabled to learn entire *word families,* a process that can dramatically expand their working vocabulary.

Categories that can be explored within a Focus on Form include *Word family and grammatical patterns; Words with the same prefix; Words with the same root;* and *Words with the same suffix.* Consider again the word *subtract:*

Word family/ grammatical patterns:	subtract, subtracts, subtracted, subtracting (verb forms)
	subtraction, subtractions (noun forms)
Words with same prefix:	substitute, subtotal, suburban, subway
Words with same root:	tractor, traction

• **Focus on Use** Students can explore the range of uses of particular words through brainstorming as a class or small group; looking words up in dictionaries, encyclopedias, or thesauri; or asking parents or other adults outside of school. Categories that can be explored within a Focus on Use include *General uses; Idioms; Metaphorical uses; Proverbs; Advertisements; Puns;* and *Jokes.* For the word *subtract,* most students will not find much that will fall within these categories other than the category of *general uses.* However, with some of the more frequent words in mathematical discourse that derive from the Anglo-Saxon lexicon of English rather than the Greek/Latin lexicon, many of these other categories will yield a multitude of examples. Consider the multiple meanings and figurative uses of words such as *great* (as in "greater than"), *big,* and *double* that students might explore.

In short, when students explore the language of mathematics by collecting specimens of mathematical language in a systematic and cumulative way, they expand not only their understanding of mathematical terms and concepts but also their knowledge of how the English language works (e.g., the fact that abstract nouns are often formed in English by adding the suffix *-tion* to the verb). The development of language awareness in this way will benefit students' reading comprehension and writing ability across the curriculum.

B. Taking ownership of mathematical language by means of "reporting back"
If students are to take ownership of mathematical language, we must provide ample opportunities and encouragement for them to use this language for authentic purposes in the classroom. In the absence of active use of the language, students' grasp of the mathematical register is likely to remain shallow and passive.

© Pearson Education, Inc., 4

Researchers (e.g., Swain, 1997) have noted three ways in which L2 acquisition is stimulated by active use of the language:

- Students must try to figure out sophisticated aspects of the target language in order to express what they want to communicate.

- It highlights to both students and teachers the aspects of language the students still find troublesome.

- It provides teachers with the opportunity to provide corrective feedback to build language awareness and help students figure out how the language works.

- **Have Students Report Back Orally and in Writing** One example of how this process operates in the teaching of content areas such as mathematics is provided by Gibbons (1991). She emphasizes the importance of *reporting back* as a strategy for promoting academic language development. For example, after a concrete, hands-on group experience or project, students are asked to report back to the class orally about what they did and observed and then to write about it. As students progress from concrete, hands-on experience to more abstract oral and written language use, they must include sufficient information within the language itself for the meaning to be understood by those who did not share in the original experience. She notes that

> while hands-on experiences are a very valuable starting point for language development, they do not, on their own, offer children adequate opportunities to develop the more 'context-free' language associated with reading and writing.... [A] reporting-back situation is a bridge into the more formal demands of literacy. It allows children to try out in speech—in a realistic and authentic situation—the sort of language they meet in books and which they need to develop in their writing. Where children's own language background has not led to this extension of oral language, it becomes even more important for the classroom to provide such opportunities (1991, p. 31).

In short, students become more aware of the cognitive processes and strategies they use to solve math problems, and they are enabled to take ownership of the language that reflects and facilitates these cognitive processes, when the curriculum provides extensive opportunities for them to explain orally and in written form what they did and how they did it.

C. Mastering the language of mathematical assessment

- **Have Students Create Test Items** High-stakes testing has become a fact of life in classrooms across the United States, and consequently a large majority of curriculum materials include not only formative assessment integrated within the curriculum unit but also practice oriented to performance on state-wide standardized tests. Consistent with the emphasis on providing opportunities for students to take ownership of the language of mathematics through active use of that language, we can also encourage students to gain insight and control over the language of mathematical assessment. We can do this by having students create their own multiple-choice (or other relevant) tests in mathematics rather than always being on the receiving end of tests that adults have created. The process might work as follows.

© Pearson Education, Inc., 4

In order to familiarize students with the process (and also have some fun in a friendly, competitive context), we can have them work in heterogeneous groups to construct their own tests, initially on topics with which they are familiar or on which they have carried out research. For example, the teacher might explain how multiple-choice items are constructed (e.g., the role of distractors), and each group might construct a set of approximately 5 items on topics such as baseball, popular music, television programs, or popular slang. These items are then pooled and the entire set of items is administered as a test to the entire class. Subsequently, each group might research aspects of a particular content area and construct items based on their research. In the context of math, groups could construct test items that focus on the unit of study (e.g., fractions or decimals) that has just been completed. An incentive system could be instituted such that the groups gain points based on their performance on the pooled test that leads ultimately to some reward.

The rationale for this reversal of roles is that construction of test items is more cognitively challenging (and engaging) than simply responding to test items. In order to come up with items that will be challenging for the other groups, students must know the content of the unit in an active rather than a passive way. The within-group discussion and collaboration in generating the items and distractors is also likely to reinforce both language and content knowledge for all students in the group, but particularly for those students (likely including some ESL students) whose grasp of the content may be fragile.

Within this conception, standardized math tests are viewed as one particular genre of math language. Students should be familiar with the conventions of this genre if their academic worth is to be recognized. In generating multiple-choice test items, students are developing language awareness in the context of a highly challenging (but engaging) cognitive activity.

The same principle can be applied to the creation of other forms of assessment that tap both math and language concepts. For example, teachers could have students create multiple-choice cloze sentences that reflect both everyday and math-specific meanings of mathematical vocabulary.

1. Five _____ six _____ eleven.
2. On the _____ side, my share _____ his.
3. On the _____ side, his share is _____ mine.
4. Numbers less than zero are called _____ numbers.
5. When we multiply by two, we _____ the quantity.

Target Words
plus
double
equals
negative

© Pearson Education, Inc., 4

Conclusion

Mathematics will assume relevance to students and be learned much more effectively when they can relate the content to their prior experience and current interests. In addition to activating students' prior knowledge and building background, we may need to modify our instruction in specific ways to make the content accessible to ESL students who are still in the process of catching up to native speakers in academic English- language proficiency. This catch-up process will typically take at least 5 years, partly because students are catching up to a moving target—native speakers of English are not standing still, waiting for ESL students to bridge the gap. Thus, even ESL students who are relatively fluent in English may require specific support in accessing mathematical concepts and problems expressed in English.

These supports should focus not only on making the mathematics content comprehensible to students but also on extending their awareness of how the language of mathematics works. In this way, students can develop insights about academic language that will bear fruit in other content areas (e.g., reading comprehension in language arts and vocabulary building in social studies). A goal of this process of extending students' command of academic language is to enable them to take ownership of the language of the curriculum and use it for authentic purposes. Thus, they will benefit from opportunities to carry out projects and explain what they did both orally and in written form. As the audience becomes more distant (e.g., in the case of a more formal written report), students are required to use more abstract, explicit, and precise language to communicate their meaning. When we integrate these active uses of language with the mathematics curriculum, students benefit both with respect to mathematics and to language facility.

References

Collier, V. P. and Thomas, W. P. (1999). Making U.S. schools effective for English language learners, Part 1. *TESOL Matters,* 9:4 (August/September), pp. 1 & 6.

Cummins (2001). *Negotiating identities: Education for empowerment in a diverse society.* 2nd edition. Los Angeles: California Association for Bilingual Education.

Díaz-Rico, L. & Weed, K. Z. (2002). *The crosscultural, language, and academic development handbook: A complete K–12 reference guide.* 2nd edition. Boston: Allyn & Bacon.

Gibbons, P. (1991). *Learning to learn in a second language.* Newtown, Australia: Primary English Teaching Association.

Meyer, L. (2000). Barriers to meaningful instruction for English learners. *Theory into Practice,* 34(2), 228–236.

Swain, M. (1997). Collaborative dialogue: Its contribution to second language learning. *Revista Canaria de Estudios Ingleses,* 34, 115–132.

© Pearson Education, Inc., 4

Numbers in the Thousands

ACCESS CONTENT

USE WITH LESSON
1-1

Objective To use place value ideas to write multiples of 100 and 1,000 in different ways.

Materials *(per group)* Set of 6 cards with 4-digit whole numbers (for example, 3,472); Place-Value Charts (Teaching Tool 1)

Vocabulary Digits, place-value chart

ESL Strategies

Use Small-Group ➤ Interactions

Use before **LEARN**

 10 MIN

Divide the class into small groups and give each group a set of cards and a place-value chart. Model the following activity for the class with the students from one group. Have a group member pick a card and write the number on the card in the place-value chart. Guide him or her in writing the digits in the proper columns on the chart. For example, if the student chooses 3,472, ask: **Which digits, or numbers, should you write in the thousands place?** *(3)* **In the hundreds place?** *(4)* **In the tens place?** *(7)* **In the ones place?** *(2)*

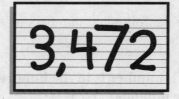

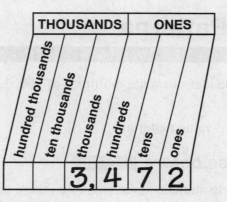

Have the student pass the chart to another group member. Invite the student to say the number aloud in word form. **How do you say this number?** *(Three thousand, four hundred seventy-two)* Encourage more advanced English speakers to help less proficient students. Have students repeat the activity until all students are comfortable writing numbers in the thousands in the place-value chart and saying them aloud in word form.

Understanding Greater Numbers

ACTIVATE PRIOR KNOWLEDGE/BUILD BACKGROUND

Objective Read and write numbers through 999,999,999.

Materials Place-Value Charts (Teaching Tool 1)

USE WITH LESSON 1-2

ESL Strategies | *Use before* **LEARN** ⏱ 10 MIN

Connect to Prior ➤
Knowledge of
Math

You know how to read and write numbers in the thousands. Write the following on the board

1,000 = one thousand   1 = one   10,000 = ten thousand

10 = ten   100,000 = one hundred thousand   100 = one hundred

Review the meanings of *greatest, greater than, less than,* and *least.* **How many numbers on the board are greater than 1,000?** *(2)* **Which numbers are less than 1,000?** *(1, 10, 100)* **Which number is greatest?** *(100,000)*

Numbers in the millions are greater than numbers in the thousands. Ask students to say the name of each column in the place-value chart from right to left. *(Ones, tens, hundreds, thousands, ten thousands, hundred thousands, millions, ten millions, hundred millions)*

Write the following numbers on the board

171,063   754   79   1,757,312

Which number is in the hundred thousands? *(171,063)* **Which number is in the millions?** *(1,757,312)*

Place-Value Patterns

USE WITH LESSON 1-3

ACCESS CONTENT

Objective Use place value ideas to write multiples of 100, 1,000, and 10,000 in different ways.

Materials Overhead place-value materials

ESL Strategies | *Use before* **LEARN** ⏱ 10 MIN

Use Manipulatives ➤

Help students understand that there are different ways to represent the same number. **You can show a number in different ways.** Place 10 tens models on the overhead. **What number is shown?** *(100)* Place a hundreds model beneath the tens models. Point to the hundreds model. **What number is shown here?** *(100)* **These models show the same number, 100. Ten tens equal one hundred.** Write 10 × 10 = 100 on the board.

Write 1,000 on the board. **How many hundreds models do we need to show this number?** *(10)* Place 10 hundreds models on the overhead. **What is**

another way to show 10 hundreds? *(With a thousands model)* Display a thousands model. **What number sentence can we write to show that 10 hundreds equal 1 thousand?** *(100 × 10 = 1,000)*

Expand Student ➤
Responses

Write 1,200 on the board. **How could you show this number?** *(With 12 hundreds models)* **How do we say this number aloud?** *(One thousand, two hundred)*

Write the following numbers on the board.

500   320   1,500   2,600

Ask volunteers to say each number in two different ways. *(Sample answers: five hundred, fifty tens; three hundred twenty, thirty-two tens; fifteen hundred, one thousand, five hundred; twenty-six hundred, two thousand, six hundred)*

Problem-Solving Skill: Read and Understand

USE WITH LESSON
1-4

ACCESS CONTENT

Objective Tell in words what is known and what needs to be determined in given word problems.

ESL Strategies

Use before CHECK ✓

⏱ 5–10 MIN

Paraphrase Ideas ➤

Write the following problem on the board.

> Sue has 15 books. Bill has 18 books. How many books do they have in all?

Ask a volunteer to read the problem aloud. **What information does the problem give you?** *(How many books each person has: Sue has 15; Bill has 18.)* **What is the question in the problem?** *(How many books do they have in all?)* **How can you answer the question?** *(Add the number of books)* **What words in the problem helped you decide?** *(How many in all)* Write the preceding four questions on the board for students to use for reference in the next activity.

Use ➤
Peer Questioning

Divide the class into pairs. Write the following problem on the board.

> Ed sees 32 red cars and 28 black cars in the parking lot. How many more red cars than black cars does Ed see?

Have one partner read the problem. Then have students take turns asking and responding to the four questions on the board. After students have identified the key information, have them work together to solve the problem. Be sure students understand that they have to subtract the black cars from the red cars. Repeat the activity, using problems from the Student Book.

Comparing and Ordering Numbers

ACCESS CONTENT

Objective Compare and order numbers through 999,999,999.

Materials *(per group)* 8 lined index cards

ESL Strategies   *Use before* **LEARN**   ⏱ 10 MIN

Use ➤ **Demonstration**

Write a 5-digit number on each of two index cards (for example, 12,561 and 15,283) and tape them on the board with the greater number on the left. Leave a space between the two numbers. **Which number is greater?** *(15,283)* **What symbol, or sign, can we write between the two numbers to show this?** Have a student write the greater than symbol *(>)* between the cards. Then have students say the comparison aloud, using the phrase *is greater than*. Tape the two cards to a different part of the board in reverse order. **Which number is less?** *(12,561)* **Which symbol can we write to compare these two numbers?** *(<)* Have students read this new comparison aloud, using the phrase *is less than*.

Use Small-Group ➤ **Interactions**

Divide the class into small groups. For each group, write eight different five-digit numbers on separate lined index cards. Use the lines as place-value columns in which to write the digits. Have students take turns shuffling the deck of number cards, picking two cards, and aligning the lines on the cards to help them compare the digits in each place. If the digits in the ten thousands place are the same, the student should compare the digits in the thousands place, and so on. Have students compare their two numbers aloud using the phrases *is greater than* or *is less than* in complete sentences. Then have every student in the group write a complete inequality sentence using the two numbers and the correct comparison symbol. Have each student take at least two turns.

Rounding Numbers

ACCESS CONTENT

Objective Round whole numbers through millions.

Materials *(per student)* Index card marked with a multiple of **10** between 3,400 and 3,500 (for example, 3,450)

Vocabulary Rounding

ESL Strategies   *Use before* **LEARN**   ⏱ 10 MIN

Use Gestures ➤

On the board, draw a number line marked off in tens that runs from 3,400 to 3,500. Then point at each tick mark while counting up the number line. Write the number 3,480 on the board. **Suppose we want to <u>round</u> a number to the nearest hundred. We should look at the second digit from the right. This is the tens digit.** Underline the tens digit: 3,4<u>8</u>0. **What is the tens digit in this number?** *(8)* Mark the location of 3,480 on the number line. **If the tens**

digit is 5 or more, do we round the number up or down? *(Up)* **So, 3,480 rounded to the nearest hundred is 3,500.** Point to 3,480 and sweep your finger up the number line to 3,500. Then write 3,430 on the board. Repeat the steps above and guide students in rounding down.

Distribute the index cards. Have each student come to the board, count by tens on the number line to write his or her number beneath the correct tick mark, and underline the digit in the tens place. Have students gesture as you did to show the direction in which they should round while they say and complete the sentence: "The tens digits is (less than 5; 5 or more), so I round (down; up)."

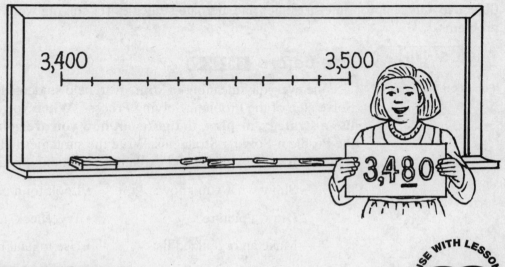

The Size of Numbers

USE WITH LESSON 1-7

ACCESS CONTENT

Objective Estimate totals made up of large numbers.

Materials 10 counters; yardstick; *(per group)* 30 counters

ESL Strategies

Use before CHECK ✓

⏱ 10 MIN

Use Demonstration ➤ Place 10 counters end to end on a desktop. Have a student use a yardstick to measure the length of the counters to the nearest foot. **Ten counters together are about 1 foot long. About how long would 100 counters be?** *(10 feet)* **1,000 counters?** *(100 feet)*

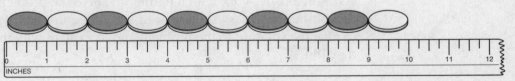

Use Manipulatives ➤ Divide the class into small groups. Give each group 30 counters. Model the activity with one group. Have a group member place several counters end to end to measure the length of a classroom object, such as a book. Have the student say and complete: "The book is about __ counters long." Then have the student ask others in the group to estimate the number of counters that would represent the combined length of large numbers of books:

"About how many counters would show the length of 100 books? 1,000 books? 10,000 books?" Students should estimate using multiples of ten. Repeat until students are comfortable using measurements of single objects to estimate measurements of large numbers of objects.

Problem-Solving-Skill: Plan and Solve

EXTEND LANGUAGE

Objective Give appropriate strategies and alernate strategies for solving word problems.

ESL Strategies

Use before CHECK ✓

⏱ 5–10 MIN

Focus on Meaning ➤ Use the everyday meaning of *strategy* to help students learn the Plan-and-Solve step of the Problem-Solving Process. **When you have a job to do, you use a strategy, or plan, to figure out how you are going to do it.** Review the Problem-Solving Strategies. Write the strategies below on the board. Read each strategy aloud and explain the meaning of each.

- Show what you know:
  - Draw a picture
  - Make an organized list
  - Make a table or chart
  - Make a graph
  - Use objects/act it out

- Look for a pattern
- Try, check, and revise
- Use logical reasoning
- Solve a simpler problem
- Work backwards
- Write an equation

Have Students ➤ Report Back Orally Write the problem below on the board. Invite a volunteer to read the problem to the class. Explain the meaning of any words or concepts students may not understand.

> It costs 75¢ to buy a can of juice from a vending machine. The machine takes only nickels and quarters. How many combinations of coins can you use to buy a can of juice from the machine?

Ask students to work with a partner to solve the problem. Tell students to use one of the strategies you reviewed and to record their work. Call on students to give the solution to the problem and to explain why they chose the strategy they did.

Using Money to Understand Decimals

ACCESS CONTENT

Objective Give money amounts in dollars, dimes, and pennies, and in ones, tenths, and hundredths.

Materials *(per student)* Bill and Coin Models (Teaching Tool 7); play money: 20 pennies, 20 dimes, 20 one-dollar bills

Vocabulary Tenth, hundredth, decimal point

ESL Strategies   *Use before* **LEARN**

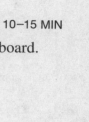 10–15 MIN

Use Graphic ➤ Organizers   Write the following pairs of problems, excluding answers, on the board. Align each pair by place value as shown.

$3.75 = *(3)* dollars + *(7)* dimes + *(5)* pennies

3.75 = *(3)* ones   + *(7)* tenths + *(5)* hundredths

$6.28 = *(6)* dollars + *(2)* dimes + *(8)* pennies

6.28 = *(6)* ones   + *(2)* tenths + *(8)* hundredths

$1.09 = *(1)* dollars + *(0)* dimes + *(9)* pennies

1.09 = *(1)* ones   + *(0)* tenths + *(9)* hundredths

Use Real Objects ➤   Have students use play money to help them find the number of dollars, dimes, and pennies in each of the money problems above. Ask volunteers to come up to the board and fill in the amounts in the money problems. Then say **Decimals can show money amounts.** Point to the corresponding digits: **A dime is one <u>tenth</u> of a dollar. This means that there are ten dimes in a dollar. A penny is one <u>hundredth</u> of a dollar. What does this mean?** *(There are one hundred pennies in a dollar.)* **We write the <u>decimal point</u> between the dollars and the cents.** Ask volunteers to fill in the decimal answers. Have students say sentences such as, "There are 2 dimes in $6.28," and "There are 5 hundredths in 3.75." Model a few examples if necessary.

Counting Money

ACTIVATE PRIOR KNOWLEDGE/BUILD BACKGROUND; ACCESS CONTENT

Objective Find the value of a given assortment of bills and coins, and tell how to make a given money amount with the fewest bills and/or coins.

Materials Overhead bills and coins; *(per pair)* Bill and Coin Models (Teaching Tool 7) or play money: pennies, nickels, dimes, quarters, one-dollar bills

Connect to Prior Experiences ➤ On the overhead, display the following arrangement of bills and coins:

Each piece of paper money is called a "bill." How do you know the value of each bill? Invite a student to come up to the overhead. He or she should point to the number on each of the bills on the overhead. **How much is each kind of coin worth?** Point to each type of coin and have students say the value of each.

Use Small-Group Interactions ➤ Have students work in pairs to think of different combinations of coins that equal the value of one dollar. *(Sample answers: 10 dimes; 2 quarters and 5 dimes; 1 quarter, 7 dimes, 1 nickel)* Ask students which combinations they found.

Use Real Objects ➤ Have pairs of students use the play money to find the total amount of money shown on the overhead. Tell them to quietly count out the money together, starting with the bills. *($17.58)* Then challenge students to use the play money to make each of the following amounts with the fewest bills and coins:

$4.28 *(4 one-dollar bills, 1 quarter, 3 pennies)*

$6.05 *(1 five-dollar bill, 1 one-dollar bill, 1 nickel)*

$25.25 *(1 twenty-dollar bill, 1 five-dollar bill, 1 quarter)*

Have students discuss how they solved the challenge.

Making Change

USE WITH LESSON
1-11

EXTEND LANGUAGE; ACTIVATE PRIOR KNOWLEDGE/BUILD BACKGROUND

Objective Make change by counting on.

Materials *(per student)* Bill and Coin Models (Teaching Tool 7) or play money

Use before LEARN

Focus on Meaning ➤ Discuss the term *making change* to help students understand how it relates to money. **Suppose you buy something at the store. You do not always have bills and coins that add up to the exact price. If you give the salesperson more money than something costs, you will get back some change. The change is the difference between the amount you gave and the price.** Provide the following example of making change on the board. Have students say each step aloud as you go over it.

> I am buying a notebook that costs $2.79. I pay with a $5 bill.

Write $2.79 on the board. **First I count on by pennies: $2.79, $2.80. I have counted on by one penny.** Write "$0.01 change" on the board beneath $2.79. **Next I count on by dimes: $2.80, $2.90, $3.00. How many dimes have I counted on?** *(2 dimes)* Write "$0.20 change" on the board. **How many dollars do I count on from $3.00 to make $5.00?** *(2 dollars)* Write "$2.00 change" on the board. **How much change do I get in all?** *($2.21)*

Use Role Playing ➤ Write the following on the board.

> You buy a backpack for $7.85. You pay with a $10 bill.
>
> You buy a CD for $12.49. You pay with a $20 bill.

Have pairs of students use play money to role-play the situations on the board. The "shopper" pays for the backpack, and the "salesperson" makes change by counting up. Then the shopper counts the change and says the total aloud. Have students reverse roles and repeat the activity with the CD example.

More About Decimals

ACCESS CONTENT

USE WITH LESSON
1-12

Objective Read, write, and shade grids to show tenths and hundredths expressed as decimals.

Materials 10 × 10 Grid Paper (Teaching Tool 5)

Use before LEARN

Give Frequent ➤ Display the following grid:
Feedback

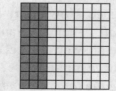

How many equal, or same, parts make up this grid? *(10 parts)* Write "ten equal parts" on the board. **How many parts are shaded, or colored in?** *(3 parts)* Write "3 shaded parts" on the board. **What fraction describes**

the shaded parts? *(Three tenths)* Write "three tenths" on the board. **What is the decimal for the shaded parts?** *(0.3)* Write 0.3 on the board.

Display the following grid and repeat the process for hundredths.

Problem-Solving Skill: Look Back and Check

ACTIVATE PRIOR KNOWLEDGE/BUILD BACKGROUND

Objective Tell whether and why the work shown for given problems is correct or not.

ESL Strategies

Use before **LEARN**   ⏱ 10 MIN

Connect to Prior
Knowledge of
Math

➤ Explain that the last step in solving a problem is to check your answer. **You check your answer to make sure that it makes sense. When an answer makes sense, we say it is reasonable. This means there is a good reason for giving that answer.**

How would you check the answer to a subtraction problem? *(By using addition)* Write 489 − 164 = 325 on the board. **What addition sentence would you write to check this answer?** *(325 + 164 = 489)* Write 325 + 164 = 489 on the board. **How would you check the answer to a multiplication problem?** *(By using division)* Write 5 × 9 = 45 on the board. **What division sentence would you use to check this answer?** *(45 ÷ 9 = 5)* Write 45 ÷ 9 = 5 on the board.

Write the following problem on the board:

> Bill has 27 baseball cards and 73 football cards. How many cards does Bill have in all?

Have a student come to the board and solve the problem by writing an addition sentence. **How many cards does Bill have in all?** *(Bill has 100 cards in all.)* Then have another student come to the board to check the answer. **Is the answer correct?** *(Yes. 100 − 27 = 73 and 100 − 73 = 27)* **Does the answer make sense? How can you tell?** *(Yes. The answer makes sense because the total number of cards is greater than the number of each type.)*

Write the following problem on the board and repeat the process with different volunteers.

Juan buys a pair of jeans for $15.75. He pays with a $20 bill. How much change should Juan receive? *(Juan should receive $4.25 in change. The answer is correct because $15.75 + $4.25 = $20.00. The answer is reasonable because the price and the change are both less than $20.00.)*

Problem-Solving Applications: Food for One Day

USE WITH LESSON 1-14

ACTIVATE PRIOR KNOWLEDGE/BUILD BACKGROUND

Objective Review and apply key concepts, skills, and strategies learned in Chapter 1.

Materials *(per group)* Bill and Coin Models (Teaching Tool 7) or play money; 30 pennies, 30 dimes, 30 dollar bills, paper and pencil

ESL Strategies

Use before **LEARN**

🕐 5 MIN

Use Role Playing ➤ Read aloud the following word problem, excluding the answer, and then write it on the board.

A soccer ball costs $9.75, a basketball costs $9.97, and a baseball costs $9.57. Order the prices from greatest to least. Which ball costs the most? *($9.97, $9.75, $9.57; the basketball costs the most.)*

Have groups of 3 students use coins and bills to act out the problem. One student shows the price of the soccer ball, another shows the price of the basketball, and a third shows the price of the baseball. Students decide the order and the most expensive ball by comparing amounts shown.

Mental Math: Adding

USE WITH LESSON 2-1

ACCESS PRIOR KNOWLEDGE/BUILD BACKGROUND; ACCESS CONTENT

Objective Compute sums of numbers mentally.

Vocabulary Breaking apart, addends, sum

ESL Strategies **Use before** **CHECK ✓**   🕐 5–10 MIN

Connect to Prior Experiences ➤ Ask students to think of everyday situations when doing math in their heads is useful for finding <u>sums</u>. *(Sample answers: adding the prices of items in a grocery store, figuring out how much time it will take to finish homework)* Students who have trouble finding sums abstractly may be able to find them more easily when the <u>addends</u> relate to familiar real-world objects and situations.

Use Small-Group Interactions ➤ Write the following on the board.

17 basketballs + 19 basketballs = ____ total basketballs

62 game points + 25 game points = ____ total game points

130 baseball cards + 75 baseball cards = ____ total baseball cards

Point to the basketball problem. **How would you solve this problem mentally, or in your head? What method can you use?** *(Sample response: <u>Break apart</u> one of the addends to make a ten.)* **What steps can you now take to find the sum?** *(Sample response: To find 17 + 19, I break apart 17 into 1 + 16. Then I add 19 + 1 = 20, and 20 + 16 = 36 basketballs.)* Divide the class into pairs. Have one partner read aloud the next problem on the board and suggest a computation method. Then have the other partner find the sum mentally and explain the steps of the given computation method, as above. Have partners switch roles for the last problem. Encourage them to suggest different methods for finding answers to the same problem.

Mental Math: Subtracting

USE WITH LESSON 2-2

ACCESS CONTENT

Objective Compute differences of numbers mentally.

Materials *(per pair)* 7 subtraction index cards

Vocabulary Difference

ESL Strategies **Use before** **CHECK ✓**   🕐 10 MIN

Use Demonstration ➤ **You can often save time and work by subtracting mentally, or in your head, without using paper and pencil.** Write the following problem on the board: 37 – 12 = ___. Point to the number 12. **Break apart 12 into 10 and 2. Then subtract each part mentally. What is 37 – 10?** *(27)* **What is 27 – 2?** *(25)* **So, what is 37 – 12?** *(25)* **What do we call the answer in a subtraction problem?** *(The <u>difference</u>)*

Use Peer Questioning ➤ Divide the class into pairs and give each pair a set of subtraction index cards. One card is marked 161, and the remaining six are marked with a subtraction sign and a subtrahend: – 7, – 9, – 12, – 99, – 136, and – 148. Have one student in each pair display the card that reads 161 and use the remaining subtraction cards as flash cards. For each subtrahend card the student displays, the partner subtracts mentally and says aloud, "The difference is ___." Encourage the pairs to check if their answers are correct. Guide partners in practicing the mental math strategies of breaking apart, compensation, and counting on as appropriate. Partners should take turns finding differences

Estimating Sums and Differences

USE WITH LESSON 2-3

ACCESS CONTENT

Objective Use rounding and front-end estimation to estimate sums and differences.

Materials Colored chalk; *(per student)* 1 index card marked with a 4-digit number

Vocabulary Rounding

ESL Strategies

Use before LEARN

🕐 15–20 MIN

Use Demonstration ➤ Using white chalk on the board, write two rows of 4-digit numbers in five columns as shown. Leave enough space between columns for students to write other numbers. Here are some pairs you might use.

4,266	1,388	2,444	7,459	3,222
2,095	6,908	5,718	1,361	9,049

Have a volunteer come to the board to <u>round</u> both numbers in the first column to the nearest hundred. Have the student explain his or her reasoning and then, using colored chalk, write the rounded numbers to the right of the original numbers.

Using the student's color of chalk, draw a line under the column of rounded numbers, and write a plus sign to the left of the bottom number. **When you estimate a sum, you need to round each of the addends to the same place. Then you add the rounded numbers. What is the estimated sum for these numbers?** *(6,400)* Have four more volunteers come to the board one at a time to round one pair of addends and find the estimated sum. Each student should use a different color of chalk.

Use Small-Group Interactions ➤ On the board, draw a number line from 1,000 to 10,000 with tick marks and values shown in increments of 1,000. Divide the class into pairs and give each student a card showing a different 4-digit number. Have each student in turn show on the number line the multiple of 1,000 to which his or her 4-digit number rounds. Then have students in each pair work together to find the sum of their two rounded numbers. Have them say the addition sentence and then write it on the board. Repeat the activity with each pair of students subtracting the lesser number from the greater number.

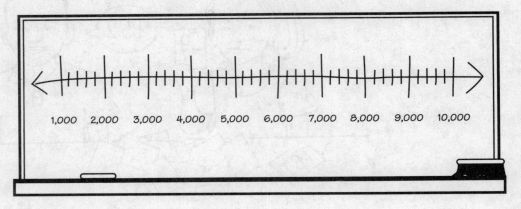

Overestimates and Underestimates

USE WITH LESSON 2-4

EXTEND LANGUAGE; ACCESS CONTENT

Objective Indicate whether an estimate is an overestimate or an underestimate.

Vocabulary Overestimate, underestimate

ESL Strategies   *Use before* **LEARN**   🕐 10–15 MIN

Focus on Meaning ➤ Help students learn about <u>overestimates</u> and <u>underestimates</u> by discussing the prefixes *over-* and *under-*. Explain that the prefix *over-* means "too much" or "too high." Discuss other words that have the prefix *over-*, such as *overdo* (do more than is necessary) and *overeat* (eat more than is healthy). So the word *overestimate* means to find an estimate that is *greater than* the exact answer. Then explain that the prefix *under-* means "too little" or "too low." Some other words that have the prefix *under-* are *underfed* (given too little to eat) and *underweight* (weighing less than is healthy). So the word *underestimate* means to find an estimate *less than* the exact answer.

Write the following on the board.

$$27 \atop +\,49$$ 　　　　 $$31 \atop +\,22$$

Use Small-Group ➤
Interactions

Have students estimate each sum and then find the exact answer. Ask volunteers to compare their estimates to the exact answers. Discuss with students how to identify an underestimate (an estimate that is less than the exact answer) and an overestimate (an estimate that is greater than the exact answer). Then have students work in pairs. Each partnership writes two problems, exchanges their problems with another pair, explains to that pair how they would use an underestimate or an overestimate to estimate each answer, and sees if that pair agrees.

Adding Whole Numbers and Money

USE WITH LESSON 2-5

ACCESS CONTENT

Objective Add and subtract whole numbers and money amounts (to five digits).

Materials *(per student)* Place-Value Blocks, Set 1 (Teaching Tool 2) or place-value models: ones, tens, hundreds; 2 teacher-made place-value charts (large enough to accommodate models)

ESL Strategies **Use before** **LEARN** ⏱ 10–15 MIN

Use ➤
Demonstration

Write "2 tens 15 ones" on the board. **We can regroup 15 ones as 1 ten 5 ones. When we do this, the number 2 tens 15 ones becomes 3 tens 5 ones. We can then rename the number in its standard, or most common, form as 35.** Write the word "rename" on the board. Point to the word and have students say it aloud. Then display 2 tens models and 15 ones models. Have a volunteer show how to regroup the models by exchanging 10 ones models for a third tens model. Have the student explain what he or she is doing, for example: "I'm regrouping 15 ones as 1 ten 5 ones. Now I have 3 tens 5 ones." **How do we rename this number in standard form?** *(35)* Then have students use the place-value blocks or models to show other regroupings. Provide examples such as "5 tens 14 ones" and "2 hundreds 12 tens 16 ones." Have students rename each number in standard form both verbally and in writing.

Column Addition

USE WITH LESSON 2-6

ACCESS CONTENT

Objective Find the sums of three or more whole numbers or money amounts.

Materials *(per group)* Teacher-made place-value chart (large enough to accommodate models); Place-Value Blocks, Sets 1 and 2 (Teaching Tools 2 and 3) or place-value models: ones, tens, hundreds, thousands

Use Manipulatives ➤ Divide the class into small groups and distribute place-value models and place-value charts. Then write the following problems on the board.

$$
\begin{array}{r} 2 \\ 21 \\ 34 \\ 8 \\ +\ 17 \\ \hline 80 \end{array}
\qquad
\begin{array}{r} 1 \\ 10 \\ 9 \\ 33 \\ +\ 21 \\ \hline 73 \end{array}
\qquad
\begin{array}{r} 1 \\ 25 \\ 31 \\ 22 \\ +\ 7 \\ \hline 85 \end{array}
$$

Point to the problems. **Remember, when you add the ones digits, or numbers, you may need to regroup 10 ones as 1 ten.** Have each group use place-value models to model the problems and the steps they used to solve them. Have one student explain each step as another student performs it. Have students take turns showing the problems and explaining the steps. For example, in the first problem: "Add 1 one, 4 ones, 8 ones, and 7 ones. The sum is 20 ones. Regroup 20 ones as 2 tens. Add the regrouped 2 tens to 2 tens, 3 tens, and 1 ten. The final sum is 8 tens, or 80."

Write the following problems, excluding answers, on the board.

$$
\begin{array}{r} 1{,}240 \\ 123 \\ +3{,}561 \\ \hline (4{,}924) \end{array}
\qquad
\begin{array}{r} 2{,}107 \\ 1{,}341 \\ +729 \\ \hline (4{,}177) \end{array}
\qquad
\begin{array}{r} 548 \\ 2{,}732 \\ +4{,}119 \\ \hline (7{,}399) \end{array}
$$

Use Gestures ➤ **When you add more than two numbers, you often use regrouping.** Point to the column for each place value in the first problem as you talk through the steps. **Which place do you add first?** *(Ones)* **Name the other places in the order in which you add them.** *(Tens, hundreds, thousands)* **First add the ones, then the tens, then the hundreds, and finally the thousands. Regroup in any place if you need to.** Have students find the answers to the problems on the board using their place-value models. Have volunteers give their answers and describe how members of their group renamed the numbers as they worked to solve the problems.

Subtracting Whole Numbers and Money

USE WITH LESSON 2-7

ACCESS CONTENT

Objective Use the standard algorithm to find differences using whole number amounts and money amounts.

Materials *(per student)* Bill and Coin Models (Teaching Tool 7) or play money

Use before LEARN

⏱ 10–15 MIN

Use Manipulatives ➤ Write the following problems, excluding answers, on the board.

$8.37	$5.46	$7.73	$6.43
-4.62	-1.87	-3.10	-5.85
($3.75)	($3.59)	($4.63)	($0.58)

When you subtract money amounts, you may need to regroup. You regroup just as you would if there were no dollar sign or decimal point.

Write "pennies," "dimes," and "dollar bills" on the board. Have students use these words to say and complete the following sentences: **The digit in the hundredths place shows the number of** *(pennies)*. **The digit in the tenths place shows the number of** *(dimes)*. **The digit in the ones place shows the number of** *(dollar bills)*.

Have students use play money to find each difference. You may want to have students use play money to solve each problem. **Make sure each difference includes both a dollar sign and a decimal point.** After students have found the four differences, have them check their answers by adding each difference and subtrahend.

Choose a Computation Method

EXTEND LANGUAGE

USE WITH LESSON
2-8

Objective For a variety of problems, state the computation method to be used and add or subtract using that method.

Materials *(per student)* Calculator

Use before LEARN

⏱ 10 MIN

Have Students ➤
Report Back
Orally

Write 175 + 239 = _____ on the board. Explain that students can use three different methods to find the sum. **You can use mental math to find the sum. You can use paper and pencil. Or, you can use a calculator.**

Have three students find the sum, each using one of the methods. Ask each student to say aloud what he or she did in order to find the sum. For example: "Using mental math, I broke apart addends. 175 = 100 + 75; 239 = 200 + 39;

100 + 200 = 300; 75 + 39 = 114; 300 + 114 = 414. Using paper and pencil, I added the digits in each place, starting with the ones. I regrouped 14 ones as 1 ten 4 ones and 11 tens as 1 hundred 1 ten. 400 + 10 + 4 = 414. Using the calculator method, I pressed the keys 1, 7, 5, +, 2, 3, 9, ENTER/=. I read the display to find the sum of 414."

Each way, or method, is useful depending on the type of problem you are solving. When would you do mental math? *(When no paper and pencil or calculator is available)* **When would you use paper and pencil?** *(When there are just a few addends or when you can regroup easily)* **When**

254	659	7.73	5,874
+150	+288	-220	-3,779
(404)	*(947)*	*(1,000)*	*(2,095)*

would you use a calculator? *(When you need to regroup many times)*

Write the following problems, excluding answers, on the board.

Divide the class into small groups of 3 or 4 students. Model the activity with one group. Have each student in that group choose a method (calculator, mental math, or paper and pencil) to solve the first problem. **What method did you use? Why did you choose that method?** *(Sample answer: I used paper and pencil because it was easy to regroup.)* Then have students solve the remaining problems in their groups. For each problem, each group should tell the class why they chose the method they did.

Problem-Solving Strategy: Look for a Pattern

USE WITH LESSON 2-9

ACCESS CONTENT

Objective Give missing numbers or figures in a pattern.

Materials Colored chalk; (per pair) counters in 4 different colors

ESL Strategies   *Use before* **LEARN**   ⏱ 10 MIN

Use ➤
Demonstration
Using colored chalk, draw a pattern of circles and stars on the board. For example, you might draw 1 circle, 1 star, 2 circles, 2 stars, 3 circles, 3 stars, and so on. **How would you describe this pattern?** *(Add 1 more circle and 1 more star each time.)*

Use ➤
Peer Questioning
Divide the class into pairs. Give each pair a supply of counters in 4 different colors. Have one student take the counters and use them to create a pattern. Patterns may be based on various combinations of color and position. Then have the other student ask his or her partner questions about the pattern to try

to determine the pattern. For example, a student might ask his or her partner, "Will the number of green counters always be the same?" or "Is a red counter always below a blue one?" Once the second student has determined and explained the pattern, have students reverse roles.

Problem-Solving Skill: Translating Words to Expressions

USE WITH LESSON 2-10

ACCESS CONTENT

Objective Write number expressions for phrases.

ESL Strategies **Use before** **LEARN**   ⏱ 5–10 MIN

Use Graphic Organizers ➤ Draw a word web on the board. Start with two center ovals, one labeled "Add" with a plus sign beneath and the other labeled "Subtract" with a minus sign beneath.

Help students brainstorm words and phrases that might go in the surrounding ovals of the web. As words and phrases are called out, add them to the web. As an alternative to having students call out words and phrases, you might have volunteers come to the board one at a time and write their suggestions directly in the web.

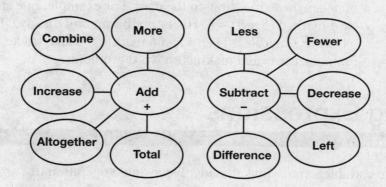

Matching Words and Number Expressions

USE WITH LESSON 2-11

ACCESS CONTENT

Objective Choose and evaluate the number expression that matches a word phrase.

Materials *(per pair)* 4 index cards

Vocabulary Parentheses

ESL Strategies **Use before** **CHECK** ✓   ⏱ 5 MIN

Expand Student Responses ➤ Write the following word problem and expressions on the board.

Ellen had 6 pencils. She gave 2 pencils to Joe. Then she bought 3 more pencils.

$$6 + (2 + 3) \qquad\qquad (6 - 2) + 3$$

Point to each part of the expressions as you explain that number expressions can include numbers, operation symbols, and <u>parentheses</u>. Point to each element of the expressions as you explain that the parentheses tell which operation to do first. Invite students to say the word *parentheses* after you.

Point to the expression on the left. **How many numbers are in this expression?** *(3)* **Are they the same numbers as the ones in the problem?** *(Yes)* **Which operation do you do first?** *(Add 2 + 3)* **How do you know?** *(They are in parentheses.)* Ask a volunteer to simplify the expression, saying the steps aloud. **Does this expression show what the words describe in the problem?** *(No)* **Why not?** *(The words say that she had 6 pencils, then gave 2 away, then got 3 more.)* **Good. What operation would show that she gave some away?** *(Subtraction)* Then point to the expression on the right, asking similar questions and expanding on students' responses. **What about this expression? Does it show what the words describe in the problem?** *(Yes. It shows that she had 6 pencils. First she gave away 2. Then she got 3 more.)*

Use Small-Group Interactions ➤ Divide the class into pairs. Give each pair a set of 4 index cards with one of these expressions on each: $(5 + 7) - 6$; $2 + (7 - 5)$; $(\$10 - \$2) - \$1$; and $\$7 - (\$4 + \$1)$. Model the activity with one pair first. Have one student hold up an index card. Then have the other student make up a simple word problem that matches the expression on the card. For example, one student holds up the card marked $(5 + 7) - 6$. His or her partner might say, "I had 5 marbles. Joe gave me 7 marbles. Then I lost 6 marbles." Have students take turns holding up index cards and making up word problems.

Evaluating Expressions

ACCESS CONTENT

USE WITH LESSON 2-12

Objective Evaluate variable expressions that involve a single operation of addition or subtraction.

Materials *(per pair)* Two-color counters; shoe box or other small box; self-stick notes; index cards marked + and −

Vocabulary Variable, evaluate an expression

ESL Strategies *Use before* LEARN 🕐 10–15 MIN

Use Demonstration ➤ Display 6 counters on a desktop. To the right of them, place the "plus" card.

Display an empty box and say: **This box can hold any number of counters. In math we can use any letter to name this box. Let's name this box "d."** Write the letter *d* on a self-stick note and attach it to the side of the box.

Use Gestures ➤ Place the box on the desktop to the right of the "plus" card and say: **This shows 6 counters *plus* a number of counters in "d." The value of the expression $6 + d$ depends on how many counters are in the box.** Place 5 counters in the box. **What is the expression now?** *(6 counters plus 5 counters)* **What is the value of the expression?** *(11 counters)* Place 2 more counters in the box and ask: **What is this expression?** *(6 counters plus 7 counters)* **What is the value of the expression?** *(13 counters)* Take all but 2 counters out of the box and ask: **Now what is the value?** *(8 counters)*

In algebraic expressions, we use a <u>variable</u> to stand for a certain number. In the expressions we just modeled, the letter *d* is the variable. It can stand for any number. If *d* stands for 5, what is the value of the expression? *(11)* **If *d* stands for 7?** *(13)* **If *d* stands for 2?** *(8)* **When we find the value of the expression, we <u>evaluate the expression</u>.**

Use Small-Group Interactions ➤ Divide the class into pairs and give each pair a set of counters, cards marked + and −, a box, and a self-stick note. Have one student in each pair use the self-stick note to label the box with a variable. Then have that student set up an algebraic expression using the labeled box, the counters, and the operation symbol cards. Direct the second student to write the expression on paper. Then have the first student suggest a number for the variable and the second student evaluate the expression. Have students reverse roles and repeat the exercise.

Solving Addition and Subtraction Equations

USE WITH LESSON 2-13

ACCESS CONTENT

Objective Find the solution to an equation informally by substituting values for the variable.

Vocabulary Equation, solution, solve

ESL Strategies   *Use before* **LEARN**   ⏱ 10 MIN

Use Pictures ➤ **In an <u>equation</u>, what must be true of the expressions on each side of the equal sign?** *(They must be equal.)* **You can think of an equation as a balance. Both sides of the equation must balance, or be the same.** Draw a simple balance scale on the board. Draw 7 squares in the first pan and 4 squares in the second pan. **Do these two groups of squares balance?** *(No)* Draw 3 more squares in the second pan. **Do the two groups of squares balance now?** *(Yes)*

Erase the squares. Write the number 7 in the first pan and the number 4 in the second pan. **Do these two numbers balance?** Encourage students to respond in complete sentences. *(No, they do not balance.)* Write + 3 after the 4 in the second pan. **Do these two numbers balance now?** *(Yes, the two numbers balance now.)* **When we** solve **an equation, we make sure that both sides are equal.**

Erase the numbers. Write the number 6 in the first pan and $4 + x$ in the second pan. Then write $x = 1$ above the second pan. **Does the equation balance if $x = 1$?** *(No, the equation does not balance.)* Change the expression above the pan to $x = 2$. **Does the equation balance if $x = 2$?** *(Yes, the equation balances.)* **2 is the solution to the equation. It is the number that balances both sides, or makes them equal.**

Write the number 2 in the first pan and $5 - x$ in the second pan. Then write $x = 1$ above the second pan. **Does the equation balance?** *(No, the equation does not balance.)* Change the expression above the second pan to $x = 2$. **Does the equation balance now?** *(No, it still does not balance.)* Change the expression above the second pan to $x = 3$ and ask: **Does the equation balance now?** *(Yes, the equation balances now.)*

Problem-Solving Applications:
Mountains

USE WITH LESSON
2-14

ACCESS CONTENT

Objective Review and apply key concepts, skills, and strategies learned in this and previous chapters.

Materials *(per pair)* Drawing paper and crayons

Vocabulary Equation, solution, solve

ESL Strategies *Use before* **LEARN**   ⏱ 5 MIN

Use Pictures ➤ Read aloud the following word problem, excluding the answer, and then write it on the board.

> John has 24 basketball cards, 14 baseball cards, 19 soccer cards, and 7 hockey cards. Which is greater, the difference between the amount of basketball cards and soccer cards, or the difference between the amount of baseball cards and hockey cards? *(the difference between the amount of baseball and hockey cards)*

Have students work in pairs, drawing pictures to help them solve the problem. They may draw the different types of cards, or they may just draw circles to represent them. Have students divide their paper into 4 sections, one for each type of card, before they start drawing.

Meanings for Multiplication

ACCESS CONTENT

Objective Recognize equal groups, repeated addition, arrays, and multiplicative comparisons as multiplication.

Materials *(per student)* 1 sheet of paper divided into 4 horizontal sections; 20 paper clips

Vocabulary Array, factor, product

ESL Strategies

Use before **LEARN**

🕙 10–15 MIN

Use Demonstration ➤ Write the word "multiplication" on the board. Beneath it, draw an <u>array</u>: 3 rows of circles with 5 circles in each row. Next to the array write "3 rows of 5." **An array can help you learn multiplication. Objects arranged in equal rows form an array. A row goes across. There are 3 rows of circles in this array. There are 5 circles in each row.** Point to the rows and the circles.

Use Manipulatives ➤ Give each student 20 paper clips and a sheet of paper divided by lines into 4 horizontal sections. Have students place 5 paper clips in each section so that they are aligned vertically and evenly spaced. **How many rows are there?** *(4)* **How many paper clips are in each row?** *(5)* **If you add 5 paper clips 4 times, how many paper clips are there in all?** *(20)*

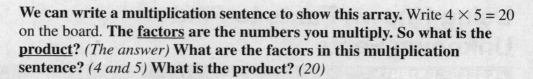

We can write a multiplication sentence to show this array. Write $4 \times 5 = 20$ on the board. **The <u>factors</u> are the numbers you multiply. So what is the <u>product</u>?** *(The answer)* **What are the factors in this multiplication sentence?** *(4 and 5)* **What is the product?** *(20)*

On the board write "2 rows of 6." **Tell me how you can arrange the paper clips to show this situation.** *(Put 6 paper clips in each of 2 rows.)* **What multiplication expression can you write to describe this array?** *(2×6)* **What are the factors?** *(2 and 6)* **What is the product?** *(12)*

Patterns in Multiplying
by 0, 1, 2, 5, and 9

USE WITH LESSON
3-2

ACCESS CONTENT

Objective Use patterns to find products with factors of 0, 1, 2, 5, and 9.

Materials *(per group)* Multiplication Chart (Teaching Tool 13) or blank multiplication facts table from 0 × 0 through 10 × 10; 100 counters

Vocabulary Zero Property of Multiplication, Identity Property of Multiplication

ESL Strategies   *Use before* **CHECK ✓**   🕐 10–15 MIN

Use Graphic Organizers ➤ Assign students to groups and give each group a blank multiplication facts table and a set of 100 counters. Draw a blank table on the board. Point to 0 × 1. **Can you use your counters to make an array that shows 0 × 1?** *(No)* **Why not?** *(You cannot make an array with 0 rows or 0 columns.)* Ask volunteers to give the product for several multiplication facts with zero. **What do you notice about the product of a number and zero?** *(The product is always zero.)* Then have students fill in the zero row on their tables as you fill in yours. **What property can help you remember these facts?** *(Zero Property of Multiplication)* Ask students to define the property in their own words. *(Sample answer: Whenever you multiply a number by zero, the answer is zero.)*

Use Small-Group Interactions ➤ Have each group make an array to represent each multiplication fact with 1, and then complete the ones row on the table. **What do you notice about the product of a number and 1?** *(The product is the same as the first number.)* Ask each group to give an answer for a fact involving 1. **What property can help you remember these facts?** *(Identity Property of Multiplication)* Have each group come up with a definition of the property in their own words. *(Sample answer: Whenever you multiply a number by 1, the answer is that number.)*

Have groups make arrays and fill in their tables for multiplication facts with 2, 5, and 9. In each case, ask volunteers to describe the patterns they see.

Using Known Facts to Find
Unknown Facts

USE WITH LESSON
3-3

ACCESS CONTENT

Objective Use the Distributive Property to find products by breaking unknown facts into known facts.

Materials 30 counters; 2 pieces of cardboard; *(per pair)* 50 counters

Use before CHECK ✓ ⏱ 5–10 MIN

Use ➤
Demonstration

On a desktop, place the two pieces of cardboard top-to-bottom and arrange 30 counters in an array of 6 rows of 5 counters so that 4 rows are on one piece of cardboard and 2 rows are on the other. Ask a volunteer to count the number of rows. *(6)* Ask another volunteer to count the number of counters in each row. *(5)* **What multiplication sentence can we write to show this array?** *(6 × 5 = 30)* Carefully pull the pieces of cardboard apart so that they are separated by several inches on the desktop. Have volunteers describe each new array. *(4 rows of 5 counters and 2 rows of 5 counters)* **What multiplication sentences can we write to find the products shown by these arrays?** *(4 × 5 = 20 and 2 × 5 = 10)* **What is the sum of these two products?** *(20 + 10 = 30)* Write 6 × 5 = 30 and (4 × 5) + (2 × 5) = 30 on the board. **If we break a factor into two parts, do we get the same answer?** *(Yes)* **Which factor in the 6 × 5 array did we break apart?** *(6)*

Use Manipulatives ➤

Divide the class into pairs and give each pair 50 counters. Write 3 × 7 on the board. Have the students work together to make an array for that fact. Then have them make two more arrays to show the factor 7 broken apart. Have them count the counters to ensure that the sum of the products modeled in the last two arrays is equal to the product modeled in the first array.

Multiplying by 10, 11, and 12

EXTEND LANGUAGE; ACCESS CONTENT

USE WITH LESSON 3-4

Objective Find products of factors of 10, 11, and 12.

Materials *(per pair)* Calculator

Use before LEARN ⏱ 5–10 MIN

Focus on Meaning ➤

Write the following pairs of problems, excluding answers, on the board. Have students find each pair of products.

5 × 1 = *(5)*   9 × 1 = *(9)*   4 × 1 = *(4)*   8 × 1 = *(8)*   10 × 1 = *(10)*

5 × 10 = *(50)* 9 × 10 = *(90)* 4 × 10 = *(40)* 8 × 10 = *(80)* 10 × 10 = *(100)*

Ask students to compare the two products in each pair. **Which factor is the same in the top row of multiplication sentences?** *(1)* **What is the rule about products when one of the factors is 1?** *(The product is equal to the other factor.)* **What is the name of the property that says the product of 1** and another number is that number? *(Identity Property of Multiplication)* **In the top row of multiplication sentences, which factor stays the same?** *(The factor that is not 1)* Then ask students to come up with more expressions that show the Identity Property of Multiplication.

Expand Student > Responses Point to the bottom row. **What is the second factor in these multiplication sentences?** *(10)* **When 10 is used as a factor, we say that the product is a multiple of 10. What other words sound like the word *multiple*?** *(Multiply, multiplication)* **Is 10 a factor in each multiplication sentence in the bottom row?** *(Yes)* **Is each product in the bottom row a multiple of 10?** *(Yes)* Ask students to compare products in the top row to products in the bottom row. Then have them describe the patterns they see in their own words.

Problem-Solving Strategy: Make a Table

ACCESS CONTENT

USE WITH LESSON

3-5

Objective Make tables and use them to solve word problems.

ESL Strategies | *Use before* **LEARN**   ⏱ 10–15 MIN

Use > Demonstration Present this word problem: **You need to buy candles and candleholders for a party. You have to buy the same number of candles and candleholders. Candles cost $1. Candleholders cost $2. You have $12.** On the board, write "Candles: $1; Candleholders: $2; You have $12." **How many candles and candleholders can you buy with $12?**

Write the following near the top of the board.

Number of Each Item = 1	Cost of Candles = ___	Cost of Candleholders = ___	Total Cost = ___

Ask students to provide the missing values. *($1, $2, $3)* Then write the following.

Number of Each Item = 2	Cost of Candles = ___	Cost of Candleholders = ___	Total Cost = ___

Ask students to provide the missing values. *($2, $4, $6)* Repeat until the total reaches $12. **How many candles and how many candleholders can you buy with $12?** *(4 candles and 4 candleholders)*

We can show this information without having to write the same words over and over. We can make a table. Create the following table on the board. Explain that each column of the table names the same things as the text you wrote on the board, and that the rows are used to show the different values. Have volunteers take turns reading the table. **How much money would you need to buy 5 candles and the same number of candleholders?** Have students create the next row of the table. *(5; $5; $10; $15)*

Number of Each Item	Cost of Candles	Cost of Candleholders	Total Cost
1	$1	$2	$3
2	$2	$4	$6
3	$3	$6	$9
4	$4	$8	$12

Meanings for Division

ACCESS CONTENT

USE WITH LESSON
3-6

Objective Use sharing and repeated subtraction to solve word problems with division.

ESL Strategies

Use before **LEARN**

⏱ 10–15 MIN

Use Total Physical Response ➤ Count the students in your class, and ask them to count along with you. If the number of students is even, write that number on the board. If the number of students is odd, count yourself as well and then write that number on the board. **We are going to practice making equal groups. Let's make two equal groups.**

Have students count off by twos (1, 2; 1, 2; etc.). If needed, join in and count yourself to make an even number. Have the 1s form one group and the 2s form another group. **Now we have 2 groups.** Have a volunteer count the number in each group. **How many people are there in each group?** Write that number on the board. **Are the two groups equal?** *(Yes)*

Have students return to their desks and count off again. If the number of students is odd, do not join the count. If the number of students is even, include yourself to make an odd number. **Are the two groups equal now?** *(No)* Remove a student (or yourself) from the larger of the two groups. **Now we have 2 equal groups and 1 person left over.** Write the number plus the remainder on the board.

Write the following sentence on the board: "With ___ people, you can make 2 equal groups of ___ people, each with ___ person left over." Slowly read aloud the sentence, pausing at the blanks.

Ask students to copy the sentence and then fill in the missing numbers using the numbers on the board. Repeat the activity, asking students to count off by 3s, 4s, and 5s. Have students adjust the sentence on the board each time.

Relating Multiplication and Division

USE WITH LESSON 3-7

ACCESS CONTENT

Objective Complete multiplication and division fact families, and write fact families for given numbers.

Materials Photographs from magazines

Vocabulary Fact family

ESL Strategies | *Use before* LEARN | 15 MIN

Use Pictures ➤ Choose photographs from magazines that can be used to illustrate a variety of situations involving multiplication and division. Alternatively, make simple drawings. Use the following example, or adapt the activity to pictures you have chosen.

Display a photo showing a pile of 24 books and an empty bookcase with 3 shelves. **A fourth-grade class has 24 new science books. The students need to put them on an empty bookcase. The bookcase has 3 shelves. How many books should the students put on each shelf so that each shelf has an equal number of books? Which operation would you use to solve this problem, multiplication or division?** *(Division)* **Which words helped you to decide which operation to use?** *("Each shelf" and "equal number")*

3 times 4 equals ...

Remind students that phrases such as *equal shares, how many, how many are left,* and so on will help them decide which operation they should choose to solve a problem. Then ask students what division sentence they might write to solve the bookcase problem. *(24 ÷ 3 = 8)* Record the sentence on the board. **So, the students should put 8 books on each shelf. What multiplication sentence can you write to tell how many books there are in all?** *(3 × 8 = 24)* Record the sentence on the board. **The sentences 24 ÷ 3 = 8 and 3 × 8 = 24 are part of the same <u>fact family</u>. What is**

a fact family? *(A set of math equations that each have the same numbers)*
What are the other sentences in this fact family? *(8 × 3 = 24,*
24 ÷ 8 = 3) Record these sentences on the board. Then point to all four
sentences. **This is the fact family for 3, 8, and 24.**

Division Facts

ACCESS CONTENT

USE WITH LESSON
3-8

Objective Divide using a related multiplication fact.

Materials 2 sets of index cards numbered 0–10; index cards marked
÷, ×, =, ?

ESL Strategies

Use Total ➤
Physical Response

Use before **LEARN**

🕐 10 MIN

**We are going to use number cards to make multiplication and division
sentences.** Ask five students to come to the front of the room. Hand each
student a card marked with one of the following numbers and symbols: 3, 2,
×, ?, and =. Arrange the five students in a line so that they display the
number sentence 3 × 2 = ? **What is the question in the number sentence
asking?** *(What is 3 times 2?)* **What is the product of 3 times 2?** *(6)* Ask a
volunteer to select the card marked with the correct product from a complete
set of number cards. Have him or her replace the student holding the
question mark. Then read the completed number sentence aloud with the
class: **3 multiplied by 2 equals 6.**

We can use what we know about multiplication to help us divide. Ask a
volunteer to take the card with the division sign and replace the student holding
the multiplication sign. Have the students holding the number cards rearrange
themselves so that they now display the number sentence 6 ÷ 2 = 3. **What
does this number sentence show?** *(6 divided by 2 equals 3.)*

Repeat using other numbers as factors and products and then as divisors,
dividends, and quotients. As each pair of related multiplication and division
sentences are formed, write them on the board.

3	**X**	**2**	**=**	**6**
6	**÷**	**2**	**=**	**3**

Special Quotients

ACCESS CONTENT

Objective Give quotients of zero when the number divided is zero, give a quotient of 1 when a number is divided by itself, and give the number divided as the quotient when dividing by 1.

Materials *(per student)* 10 counters; 10 paper cups

ESL Strategies — ***Use before*** **LEARN**   ⏱ 5–10 MIN

Use Manipulatives ➤ Write 1×1 on the board. Have each student use the paper cups to model dividing 1 counter into 1 group. **How many counters do you use?** *(1)* **How many cups do you need?** *(1)* **How many counters are in each cup?** *(1)* **So, what is the answer to $1 \div 1$?** *(1)* Finish writing the number sentence to show $1 \div 1 = 1$. Repeat the procedure using $2 \div 1$, $3 \div 1$, $4 \div 1$, and so on through $10 \div 1$. Ask students to look for a pattern. *(Any number divided by 1 is that number.)* **You have just stated a rule of division.**

Write $2 \div 2$ on the board. Have each student model dividing 2 counters into 2 groups. Then finish writing the number sentence to show $2 \div 2 = 1$. Repeat the procedure using $3 \div 3$, $4 \div 4$, $5 \div 5$, and so on through 10×10. Ask students to look for a pattern. *(Any number divided by itself is 1.)* **This division rule works for all numbers except zero.**

Write $3 \div 0 = ?$ on the board. Ask a student to explain what this number sentence is asking. *(What is 3 divided by 0?)* Have students try to divide 3 counters into 0 groups. **Can you divide 3 counters into 0 groups?** *(No)* **Why not?** *(Sample answer: As long as you have any counters, you have one group.)* **You cannot divide any number by 0. This is another rule of division.**

Write $0 \div 5 = ?$ on the board. Ask a student to explain what this number sentence is asking. *(What is 0 divided by 5?)* Have students try to divide 0 counters into 5 groups. **Can you divide 0 counters into 5 groups?** *(No)* **Why not?** *(Sample answer: Because zero cannot be broken apart)* **If zero cannot be broken apart, then what is $0 \div 5$?** *(0)* **The last rule of division says that zero divided by any number (except 0) is 0.**

Multiplication and Division Stories

ACTIVATE PRIOR KNOWLEDGE/BUILD BACKGROUND

Objective Write stories using given multiplication and division facts.

Materials *(per pair)* 30 Power Polygons (assorted shapes)

ESL Strategies — ***Use before*** **CHECK**   ⏱ 15 MIN

Use Role Playing ➤ Assign students to groups of 3. If possible, group together English learners who share the same primary language. Model the activity with one group.

Have one student use Power Polygons to create a situation for related multiplication and division problems. Another student then tells and solves a multiplication story for those shapes. The third student tells and solves a division story for those shapes.

For example: Student 1 makes 2 groups of 5 shapes each. Student 2 says, "You made 2 groups of shapes. There are 5 shapes in each group. How many shapes are there in all? There are 10 shapes in all." Student 3 says, "There are 10 shapes divided into 2 equal groups. How many shapes are in each group? There are 5 shapes in each group."

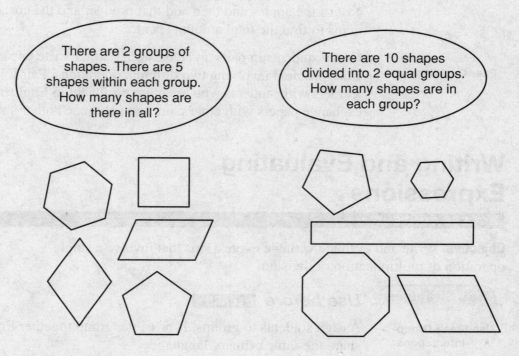

There are 2 groups of shapes. There are 5 shapes within each group. How many shapes are there in all?

There are 10 shapes divided into 2 equal groups. How many shapes are in each group?

Have students in each group switch roles so that each has a turn making groups, telling a multiplication story, and telling a division story.

Problem-Solving Skill: Multiple-Step Problems

USE WITH LESSON **3-11**

ACTIVATE PRIOR KNOWLEDGE/BUILD BACKGROUND; ACCESS CONTENT

Objective Solve multiple-step word problems.

ESL Strategies

Use before **LEARN**

⏱ 10 MIN

Connect to Prior ➤ Knowledge of Math

Write the following sentences on the board: "Bill went to the store. He bought three apples for $1.00 each. How much did he spend?" *($3.00)* **You are familiar with this type of problem. How would you solve it?** *(By multiplying $1.00 by 3)*

Now write the following sentences on the board as a separate problem: "Bill bought a quart of milk for $1.65 and a box of fruit bars for $2.49. How much did he spend?" *($4.14)* **You are also familiar with this type of problem. How would you solve it?** *(By adding $1.65 and $2.49)*

We can put these two problems together to form one problem. Change the sentences on the board to read: "Bill went to the store. He bought three apples for $1.00 each. He also bought a quart of milk for $1.65 and a box of fruit bars for $2.49. How much did Bill spend altogether?" *($7.14)* **It takes more than one step to solve this problem. It is called a *multiple-step problem*. What do you think *multiple* means?** *(More than one)* **How would you solve it?** Help students understand that they should multiply to find the cost of the apples and then add that product and the costs of the other two items to find the total amount spent.

Use ➤
Peer Questioning

Group students in pairs and have each partner write one step of a two-step word problem involving two different operations. Pair English language learners with students who are more proficient in English. Then have students exchange papers with other pairs and solve each other's word problems.

Writing and Evaluating Expressions

USE WITH LESSON

3-12

ACCESS CONTENT

Objective Write and evaluate variable expressions that involve a single operation of multiplication or division.

ESL Strategies   ***Use before*** **LEARN**   ⏱ 5–10 MIN

Use Small-Group ➤
Interactions

Assign students to groups. If possible, group together English learners who share the same primary language.

Write $x + 7$ on the board. **What is the value of this expression if x equals 3?** *(10)* Have group members discuss the problem and together arrive at an answer, then write it down. Repeat the activity for $x = 2$ *(9)* and $x = 9$ *(16)*.

Write $22 - r$ on the board. **What is the value of this expression if r equals 1?** *(21)* Again, have group members discuss the problem, arrive at an answer, and write it down. Repeat the activity for $r = 11$ *(11)* and $r = 5$ *(17)*.

Write $5 \times d$ on the board. **What is the value of this expression if d equals 2?** *(10)* Have group members discuss the problem and find a solution. If any group has difficulty, have members of that group describe the process they used to evaluate the addition and subtraction expressions. Then have them apply the same process to this multiplication expression. Repeat the activity for $d = 3$ *(15)* and $d = 4$ *(20)*.

Find a Rule

EXTEND LANGUAGE

USE WITH LESSON 3-13

Objective Find the rule for a pattern presented in a table, and use the rule to add inputs and outputs to the table.

ESL Strategies | **Use before** LEARN   ⏱ 5 MIN

Focus on Meaning ➤ **Rules tell us about things we must do. We also use rules in math. For example, a rule can tell us how to make a pattern.** Write the pattern below on the board.

> 2, 4, 6, 8, 10, 12

Look at the number pattern. What can we do to get from 2 to 4? *(Add 2)* **To get from 4 to 6?** *(Add 2)* **From 6 to 8?** *(Add 2)* **From 8 to 10?** *(Add 2)* **From 10 to 12?** *(Add 2)* **We can add 2 to get from one number to the next. So what is the rule for making this pattern?** *(Add 2 to each number.)* **Other patterns may use subtraction, multiplication, or division.**

Have Students ➤ Write 2, 4, 8, 16, 32, 64 on the board and ask students to work with a partner
Report Back to discover the rule for the pattern. Call on students to report back by telling
Orally what rule the pattern uses and then explaining orally why that is the correct rule. *(Multiply by 2; to get from 2 to 4, from 4 to 8, from 8 to 16, and so on, you must multiply by 2 each time.)*

Solving Multiplication and Division Equations

ACCESS CONTENT

USE WITH LESSON 3-14

Objective Find the solution to an equation by testing a set of values for the variable.

Vocabulary Equation

ESL Strategies | **Use before** LEARN   ⏱ 5–10 MIN

Use Pictures ➤ Draw a balance with 4 circles in one pan and the number 12 on the other pan.

This balance shows that both sides are the same. **How many circles are shown in the left pan of the balance?** *(4)* **What number is shown in the right pan?** *(12)* How can we write a number sentence to describe what is shown on the balance?

Write ___ = ___ on the board.

We are writing an <u>equation</u>**. What goes on the left side of the equal sign?** *(4 circles)* **What goes on the right side?** *(12)* **Let's use a variable to stand for a circle.** Ask a volunteer to choose a letter, for example, *n*. **If *n* equals 1 circle, how many *n*'s do we need to equal 12?** *(4)*

On the left of the equal sign, write 4 *n*'s with spaces between them. Write the numeral 12 on the other side. **What's a better way to show that there are 4 *n*'s altogether?** *(Write a plus sign between each.)* Insert the plus signs into the equation: $n + n + n + n = 12$. **What number for *n* would make the sentence true?** *(3)* **How many 3s are in 12?** *(4)* **What multiplication sentence shows this?** *(4 × 3 = 12)* Remind students that they found that *n* stands for 3 in this equation. **Can we also write 4 × *n* = 12?** *(Yes)* **Another way to write 4 times *n* is 4*n*.** Write $4n = 12$ on the board. **So, our equation is now 4*n* = 12.**

Have student pairs create drawings to help them in solving each of the following equations with substitution:

$$2s = 6 \qquad 3t = 9 \qquad 4w = 8$$

Problem–Solving Applications: Sleeping Animals

USE WITH LESSON 3-15

ACCESS CONTENT

Objective Review and apply key concepts, skills, and strategies learned in this and previous chapters.

Materials *(per student)* 40 paper clips

ESL Strategies | ***Use before*** **LEARN**   ⏱ 10–15 MIN

Use Real Objects ➤ Read aloud the following word problem, excluding the answer, and then write it on the board.

> **Karla has 3 times as many marbles as Jan. If Jan has 5 marbles, how many marbles does Karla have?** (15 marbles)

Have students work in pairs, using paper clips to help them solve the problem. Each student should write "Jan" at the top of his or her paper, and "Karla" about half-way down. Then he or she should use the clips to first show the number of marbles Jan has and the number of marbles Karla has.

Telling Time

EXTEND LANGUAGE

USE WITH LESSON **4-1**

Objective Tell time to the nearest 1 minute and 5 minutes using analog and digital clocks, and identify time as A.M. or P.M.

Materials *(per student)* Blank Clock Face (Teaching Tool 47)

ESL Strategies | ***Use before*** **LEARN** | 🕐 10–15 MIN

Have Students Report Back in Writing ➤ Write 8:30 on the board and show 8:30 on a clock face. **Show this time on your clock. One way to say this time is half-past eight. What is another way to say this time?** *(Eight thirty; thirty minutes after eight)* On the board, write the three different ways mentioned in words.

Write 11:20 and 3:50 on the board. Have students model each time on their clocks. Ask students to think of different ways to say these times. For example, point to 11:20 and ask students, **How many minutes after 11 is this time?** *(20 minutes)* **One way to say this time is twenty minutes after 11.** Write the different ways to say the times in words on the board. Then model 6:30, 1:05, and 3:25 on a clock face. Have students write at least two ways to say each time. They can write these entries in their math journals or as part of a bulletin-board display. Help English language learners with spelling and concepts. Invite volunteers to read what they wrote to the class.

Units of Time

ACCESS CONTENT

USE WITH LESSON **4-2**

Objective Convert among different units of time, and compare measurements of time.

Vocabulary Minute, hour

ESL Strategies | ***Use before*** **LEARN** | 🕐 5–10 MIN

Use Graphic Organizers ➤ Draw a table on the board as shown.

Activity	Hours	Minutes

Help students brainstorm activities that take about 1 <u>hour</u>, 2 hours, 3 hours, and so on. As activities and estimated times in whole hours are called out, insert them in the appropriate parts of the table. Then help students convert each time in hours to a time in <u>minutes</u>, inserting each conversion in the Minutes column of the table. **How many minutes are in 1 hour?** *(60)* **In 2 hours?** *(120)* **In 3 hours?** *(180)* As an alternative to having students call out activities and times, you might have volunteers come to the board one at a time and write their suggestions directly in the table.

Elapsed Time

ACCESS CONTENT

USE WITH LESSON 4-3

Objective Find elapsed time, starting time, or ending time, given two of these.

Vocabulary Elapsed time

ESL Strategies | ***Use before*** **CHECK** ✓ | ⏱ 5 MIN

Expand Student ➤
Responses

<u>Elapsed time</u> **is the amount of time that goes by between the time something starts and the time it ends.** Write "Start: 11:00 A.M." above "Finish: 1:15 P.M." on the board. Then describe the following scenario to students and ask questions as appropriate.

Suppose you go see a movie. The movie starts at 11:00 A.M. and ends at 1:15 P.M. How can we figure out how long the movie lasted? *(First count on by hours, then count on by minutes.)* **How many hours is it from 11:00 A.M. to 1:00 P.M.?** *(2 hours)* **How many minutes is it from 1:00 P.M. to 1:15 P.M?** *(15 minutes)* **How long did the movie last?** *(2 hours, 15 minutes)*

Problem-Solving Skill: Writing to Compare

EXTEND LANGUAGE

USE WITH LESSON 4-4

Objective Write comparison statements using data from tables and graphs.

ESL Strategies | ***Use before*** **LEARN** | ◕ 10–15 MIN

Focus on Meaning ➤

Write the following movie schedule on the board.

Movie Schedule

Movie	Starts	Ends
A	2:30	4:00
B	3:00	5:00
C	3:30	5:00

Have students examine the schedule. **Does Movie B start before or after Movie A?** *(After)* **We can also say Movie B starts later. Which movies start before Movie C?** *(Movies A and B)* **We can also say Movies A and B start earlier. Which two movies take the same amount of time, or last the same number of hours and minutes?** *(Movies A and C)* Invite volunteers to make statements that compare the movie data. Encourage them to use comparison words such as *later, earlier, same, more time than,* and *less time than.*

Calendars

ACCESS CONTENT

USE WITH LESSON 4-5

Objective Find dates on a calendar that are certain numbers of weeks before and after given dates.

Materials Current year's calendar

ESL Strategies *Use before* **LEARN** ⏱ 10 MIN

Use Demonstration ➤ Display each month of this year's calendar. **Who has a birthday in January?** Have any students with January birthdays circle the date on the calendar and write their names in that square. **What is the date one week before (Student's) birthday?** Model how to count back one week. **What is the date two weeks after (Student's) birthday?** Model how to count forward two weeks. Then ask other students to circle their birthdays and write their names on the calendar. Have them ask the class to answer questions such as the following:

The date of my birthday is (January 11). What is the date two weeks before my birthday? What is the date three weeks after my birthday?

Pictographs

ACCESS CONTENT

USE WITH LESSON 4-6

Objective Read, interpret, and make pictographs.

Materials 12 books

Vocabulary Pictograph, key

ESL Strategies *Use before* **LEARN** ⏱ 10–15 MIN

Use Graphic ➤ Draw the chart below on the board using the names of students in your class
Organizers instead of "Student A" and so on. **We are going to make a pictograph. A pictograph shows how many using pictures, or symbols. The key tells you how many things each picture, or symbol, stands for.**

Each ○ stands for 1 book.

Paperback Books	
Student	Number of Books
Student 1	
Student 2	
Student 3	

Use Real Objects ➤ Give Student A 4 books, Student B 6 books, and Student C 2 books. Ask Student A to bring his or her books to the front of the room. Have Student A count aloud each of his or her books and place them in a stack on your desk. As Student A counts each book, draw a circle in the appropriate place on the pictograph. Repeat with Students B and C. **How many books does (Student A) have?** *(4 books)* **(Student B)?** *(6 books)* **(Student C)?** *(2 books)* **What do you notice about the number of books and the number of circles in the pictograph?** *(The number of books and the number of circles are the same.)* **What does each circle stand for in this pictograph?** *(1 book)*

Have the 3 students retrieve their books. Erase the symbols and change the key to read "Each circle stands for 2 books." This time have the same three students count out their books by twos. For each pair of books, draw a circle in the appropriate place on the pictograph. **What does each circle stand for in this pictograph?** *(2 books)*

Draw another pictograph on the board with the students' names and the key "Each circle stands for 4 books." **Look at the pictograph that we just made. How many books does (Student A) have?** *(4 books)* **If I want to show that (Student A) has 4 books in this new pictograph, how many circles should I draw?** *(1 circle)* Direct students' attention to the key if they are uncertain. Draw 1 circle in the appropriate place in the new pictograph. **How many books does (Student B) have?** *(6 books)* **We already know that 1 circle is 4 books.** Draw 1 circle in the appropriate place. **How many circles do I draw to show 2 books?** Help students come to the conclusion that if 1 circle equals 4 books, half a circle equals 2 books. Add half a circle to the pictograph. **What should I draw to show (Student C's) books?** *(A half circle)* Draw a half circle in the appropriate place. **What does each circle stand for in this pictograph?** *(4 books)* **Each half circle?** *(2 books)*

Line Plots

USE WITH LESSON 4-7

ACCESS CONTENT

Objective Read, interpret, and make line plots.

Materials (per pair) Bag containing between 20 and 30 Two-color counters

Vocabulary Line plot, outlier

Use before `LEARN`

Use ➤
Manipulatives

A <u>line plot</u> shows how many times each number occurs in a set of data. On the board, draw a line plot that ranges from 5 to 45.

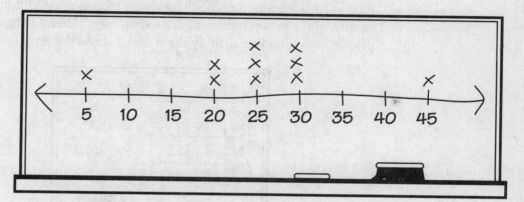

Group students in pairs and give each pair a bag of counters. Make sure one or two of the bags have totals far outside the range of 20 to 30 counters. **Count the number of counters in your bag.**

After students have finished counting, ask each pair for their total. Place Xs above the appropriate tick marks on the line plot. If a pair has an unusually small or large total, ask what is different about the total. **Does this X go in the same place as most of the other Xs?** *(No)* **When a number in a set of data is very far from the other numbers, we call it an <u>outlier</u>.** Invite students to repeat the word after you. **It lies outside the place where the other data are.** Have volunteers complete sentences such as "_____ is an outlier, because it is much less than the other numbers" and "_____ is an outlier, because it is much greater than the other numbers."

Bar Graphs

ACCESS CONTENT

USE WITH LESSON
4-8

Objective Read, interpret, and make bar graphs.

Materials (per group) Teacher-made grid paper marked in 1-inch boxes; crayons or markers

Vocabulary Bar graph, scale

Use before `LEARN`

Use Small-Group ➤
Interactions

Hold up an example of a <u>bar graph</u>. **We can use a bar graph to show data. You are going to make a bar graph to show how many people there are in your family. Then you will use the bar graph to talk about the data.**

Assign students to groups and give each group a sheet of grid paper. Demonstrate how to write the <u>scale</u> on the graph by numbering the lines along one side from 0 to 8 (or however many are needed to include the largest family). **This is the scale. It tells how many people each bar will show.**

Distribute crayons or markers to each group. Have each student draw and color a bar on the grid to show how many people are in his or her family. Remind students to include themselves when they count the members of their family. Have group members draw their bars side by side. When all the graphs are complete, display them and discuss the data.

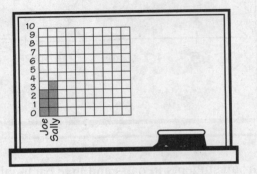

Graphing Ordered Pairs

USE WITH LESSON 4-9

ACCESS CONTENT

Objective Locate and graph ordered pairs on a coordinate grid.

Materials Map of your state; large sheet of paper; *(per pair)* index card

Vocabulary Coordinate grid

ESL Strategies

Use before **LEARN**

⏱ 10–15 MIN

Use ➤ Demonstration

Trace the outline of your state from a map onto a large sheet of paper. Add grid lines at regular, appropriately sized intervals. Label the horizontal grid lines with letters starting with A at the top. Label the vertical grid lines with numbers starting with 1 at the left. Mark and label a number of cities and towns that fall at or near the intersection of two grid lines. Finally, write the coordinates of a different city or town on each index card.

Display the map that you created. Explain that it uses a <u>coordinate grid</u> of lines that are marked with numbers and letters. Invite students to say the words coordinate grid after you. **This grid helps people find cities and towns on the map. Suppose I know that a town called (name of town) is located at point 5D. I can use the grid to find it.** Demonstrate using the lines. **Here is 5.** Trace the vertical line up with a finger on one hand. **And here is D.** Trace the horizontal line across with a finger on the other hand. **The two lines cross at this point.** Bring your fingers together to show the point. **What is this point?** *(5D)* **What does it show?** *(Name of town)*

Use Small-Group ➤ Interactions

Divide the class into pairs and distribute the index cards. Call each pair up to the map. Have the students read the coordinates on their card aloud. Then have one student trace along the number grid line and the other student trace along the letter grid line to locate the city or town on the map.

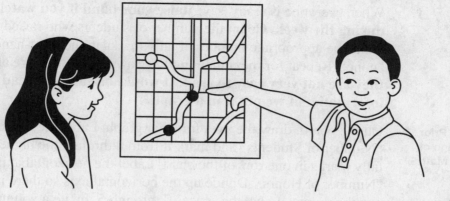

Line Graphs

ACCESS CONTENT

Objective Interpret and make line graphs.

Materials *(per student)* 1/4-Inch Grid Paper (Teaching Tool 4)

Vocabulary Line graph

ESL Strategies

Use ➤
Peer Questioning

Use before CHECK ✓

⏱ 10–15 MIN

Have each student draw and label a <u>line graph</u>. Tell students that their line graphs can describe any change over time, but be prepared to make suggestions, for example, a person's height, the number of items in a student's collection, or a store's sales over time.

Group students in pairs. Have one student in each pair display his or her line graph then ask the other student several questions about it. The student might ask, for example, "How much money did the store make in the third month?" Have his or her partner answer the questions. Then have the partners reverse roles and repeat the activity.

Problem-Solving Strategy: Make a Graph

ACTIVATE PRIOR KNOWLEDGE/BUILD BACKGROUND

Objective Use data in tables and tally charts to make line graphs, bar graphs, and pictographs to solve problems.

Materials Chalk (in 6 different colors, if possible)

ESL Strategies

Connect to Prior ➤
Experiences

Use before LEARN

⏱ 10–15 MIN

Draw a two-column tally chart on the board. Label the left-hand column "Number of Hours" and the right-hand column "Number of Students." Label the rows "none," "1 hour," "2 hours," "3 hours," "4 hours," and "5 hours." **I want to know how many hours of television students in this class watch each night during the week. Take a minute to figure out the number of hours you usually spend watching TV on a weeknight.**

When everyone is ready, say: **Raise your hand if you watch no television during the week.** Count the number of students who raised their hands and make the appropriate number of tally marks in the right-hand column next to "none." Repeat for the remaining five rows. **Now we have all the data, but they are not very easy to read. It would be easier to read this information if we put it in a graph.**

Connect to Prior Knowledge of Math ➤ On the board, draw the axes for a bar graph. Label the vertical scale "Number of Students" and mark it from 0 through the highest number of tally marks in one row of the chart. Label the horizontal axis of the graph "Number of Hours." Divide up the horizontal axis so there is space for six equal columns. Label the spaces 0 through 5. Invite a volunteer to come up to the board, select a row of the tally chart, and use the data to draw and color in a bar, or column, on the bar graph. Continue calling on volunteers until the graph is complete.

Median, Mode, and Range

ACCESS CONTENT

USE WITH LESSON
4-12

Objective Find the median, mode, and range for a given set of data.

Materials *(per group)* 30 paper clips; 4 index cards

Vocabulary Median, mode, range

ESL Strategies ⟩ *Use before* **CHECK** ✓   ⏱ 10 MIN

Use Manipulatives ➤ Divide the class into four groups. Model this activity with one group. Display one group of 5 paper clips, one group of 3 paper clips, one group of 7 paper clips, and two groups of 6 paper clips each. **How many paper clips are in each group?** *(5, 3, 7, 6, 6)* Write the numbers on the board. **How can we find the difference between the greatest number of clips in a group and the least number of clips in a group?** *(Subtract 3 from 7.)* **In a data set, that is called the <u>range</u>. What is the range of the number of paper clips in these groups?** *(4)*

List the numbers on the board in order from least to greatest: 3, 5, 6, 6, 7. Point to the first 6. **When the data are in order from least to greatest, the number in the middle is called the <u>median</u>. What is the median number of paper clips in these groups?** *(6)*

How do you find the <u>mode</u>? *(You look for a number that appears more times than the other numbers.)* **Suppose all the numbers in a data set appear the same number of times. What can you conclude?** *(There is no mode.)* **Do you see a number more than once in this list?** *(Yes)* **What is it?** *(6)*

Distribute paper clips to each group. Write one of the following sets of numbers on each of the index cards.

$$5, 7, 2, 4, 5$$

$$4, 2, 6, 8, 2$$

$$10, 1, 5, 4, 1$$

$$3, 7, 5, 4, 9$$

Have one student from each group pick a card and arrange paper clips into 5 groups to match the numbers in the set. Then have the other students in the group count the numbers of clips and describe how they will use the values to find the range, median, and mode of the data set. Have group members reverse roles and repeat the activity.

Data from Surveys

ACCESS CONTENT

USE WITH LESSON
4-13

Objective Interpret survey results and make predictions based on those results.

Materials *(per group)* Teacher-made chart of the days of the week; calendar for current year

Vocabulary Survey

ESL Strategies

Use before LEARN

⏱ 10–15 MIN

Use Graphic ➢
Organizers
Create a chart with two columns. Label the left-hand column "Days of the week" and the right-hand column "Number of students." Create a row in the chart for each day of the week. Divide the class into groups. Give each group a chart and a calendar. **We are going to take a <u>survey</u> to find out on what day of the week everyone's birthday is this year. We will use the chart to keep track of our findings. How can you find out on what day of the week your birthday is?** *(By checking a calendar)* **Look at the calendar and find out on what day of the week your birthday is this year.**

Have one member of each group give the survey and ask each of the other members on what day of the week his or her birthday is. The student then puts a tally mark in the appropriate box on the chart.

Use Small-Group ➢
Interactions
When the groups have finished their surveys, say, **I am going to ask each group to give me its data. I will collect them into a survey for the whole class.** One by one, have a student from each group read the data to you. Make a tally chart on the board and mark the appropriate tallies. When the class survey is complete, discuss the results. Ask students questions such as "How many students have birthdays on Monday?", "On what day of the week do most students have their birthdays?", and "If three more students have their birthdays on Thursday, how many students in all have their birthdays on Thursday?"

Misleading Graphs

EXTEND LANGUAGE

Objective Recognize misleading graphs and identify the misleading characteristics.

Materials *(per student)* Teacher-made grid paper marked in 1-inch boxes; crayons or markers

Vocabulary Scale

ESL Strategies

Use before CHECK ✓

⏱ 10–15 MIN

Focus on ➤ Meaning

Review the meaning of the term *misleading graphs.*

What can make a graph misleading? Describe ways that someone can show information on a graph to make you think the wrong thing. *(By not having the* <u>scale</u> *start at zero, or by using a scale whose numbers are too close or too far apart)*

Draw the following graph on the board.

This graph shows the election results for class president. How many votes did Jack receive? *(10)* **How many votes did Maria receive?** *(20)* **Why is this graph misleading? What does it make you think?** *(That Maria received 6 times as many votes as Jack, when she really received only twice as many)* **Why does it seem this way?** *(The scale does not start at zero.)*

Have students draw a new graph for the misleading one. Ask them to use the same scale, by 2s, but to start the scale at zero. Then ask volunteers to explain why their new graph gives a more accurate picture of the election results.

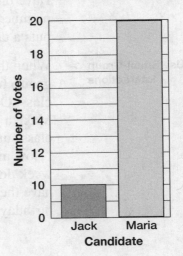

Votes for Class President

Problem-Solving Applications: Tsunamis

ACCESS CONTENT

Objective Review and apply key concepts, skills, and strategies learned in this and previous chapters.

Materials *(per student)* Clock face

ESL Strategies

Use before LEARN

⏱ 5 MIN

Use Manipulatives ➤ Read aloud the following word problem, excluding the answer, and then write it on the board.

Jenny started doing her homework at 5:15 p.m. She finished at 5:50 p.m. How much time had elapsed? *(35 minutes)*

Have students work in pairs, using their clock faces to help them solve the problem. Students set their clocks at 5:15 and then count by fives to 5:50 to find the elapsed time.

Multiplying by Multiples of 10, 100, or 1,000

ACCESS CONTENT

Objective Multiply any number by 10, 100, or 1,000.

Materials Calculator

Vocabulary Product

ESL Strategies | **Use before** | **LEARN** | 🕐 10 MIN

Use Demonstration ➤ Write $4 \times 8 = 32$ on the board. Then write the left side of the other 3 equations shown below. Ask a student to use a calculator to find the <u>products</u>. Write the products on the board to complete the equations. Then draw a think cloud as shown below to demonstrate how to to find 4×80 by multiplying a familiar fact by 10.

4×8	$= 32$
4×80	$= 320$
4×800	$= 3{,}200$
$4 \times 8{,}000$	$= 32{,}000$

Use Gestures ➤ In each of the last 3 equations, cover up the zeros on each side of the equation. **What do you notice?** *(4 × 8 on the left side equals 32 on the right side each time.)* Then for each equation, cover up the 4 × 8 and the 32. **What do you notice?** *(The number of zeros is the same on both sides.)*

Now repeat the process with these equations:

4×5	$= 20$
4×50	$= 200$
4×500	$= 2{,}000$
$4 \times 5{,}000$	$= 20{,}000$

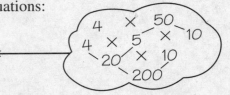

Is the number of zeros the same on both sides? *(No)* **Why?** *(There is one more zero on the right because 4 × 5 = 20.)*

Estimating Products

EXTEND LANGUAGE

Objective Use rounding and compatible numbers to estimate products.

Vocabulary Compatible numbers

ESL Strategies | **Use before** | **LEARN** | 🕐 5 MIN

Focus on Meaning ➤ Use the everyday meaning of *compatible* to help students learn the mathematical meaning of <u>compatible numbers</u>. **People who get along well**

together are compatible people. When a TV and VCR work together, they are compatible machines. In mathematics, compatible numbers are numbers that are easy to compute mentally.

Write the following on the board.

$$200 + 600 \qquad 853 - 678 \qquad 3 \times 500 \qquad 7 \times 657$$

Have Students ➤ **Take a moment to try to find the values of these expressions mentally.**
Report Back **Which expressions use compatible numbers?** *(200 + 600; 3 × 500)*
Orally **Which expressions do not use compatible numbers?** *(853 − 678; 7 × 657)*
Have volunteers explain how they found the values of the expressions with compatible numbers.

Write 4 × __ on the board and ask students to work with a partner to fill in the blank with numbers that are compatible with 4. Call on students to report back the numbers they chose, and why they think those numbers are compatible with 4.

Mental Math

USE WITH LESSON 5-3

ACTIVATE PRIOR KNOWLEDGE/BUILD BACKGROUND

Objective Mentally multiply two-digit numbers by one-digit numbers by using the Distributive Property.

ESL Strategies *Use before* **CHECK** ✓ ⏱ 10 MIN

Connect to Prior ➤ Help students do mental computation by connecting the exercise to everyday
Experiences experiences in which students might use mental computation, such as shopping. Students who have trouble finding answers using abstract numbers may be able to find answers more easily when the numbers relate to a situation involving money.

Draw sketches of these common objects and write prices by them.

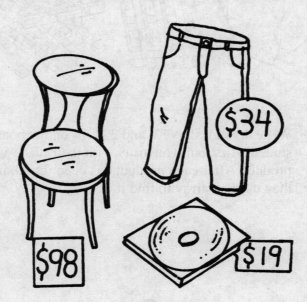

Use Role Playing ➤ Have student pairs role-play shopping in a store. One student plays the role of a shopper, and the other student plays the role of a salesperson. The shopper points to an item and says how many he or she wants. (It must be a number between 2 and 9.) Students should write a multiplication sentence for the problem. For example, to buy 3 chairs, he or she should write 3 × $98. Then the salesperson tells what the total cost is and explains how to find the answer using mental math. For example, to find 3 × $98: "I add 2 to $98 to make $100 and substitute $100 for $98. I calculate 3 × $100 = $300. Since I added 3 groups of 2, I now have to subtract 3 groups of 2: $300 − $6 = $294."

Using Arrays to Multiply

USE WITH LESSON 5-4

ACCESS CONTENT

Objective Make arrays with place-value blocks to find products

Materials *(per student)* Place-value models: 9 tens, 9 ones

ESL Strategies **Use before** **LEARN** 🕐 10–15 MIN

Use Demonstration ➤ Write 3 × 12 on the board. Use place-value models to build an array. **First I will show 3 rows with 1 ten and 2 ones in each.** Break apart the array. **Next I will break apart the array into ones and tens.** Demonstrate how to find the product. **Finally, I will add the tens and ones and give the product.**

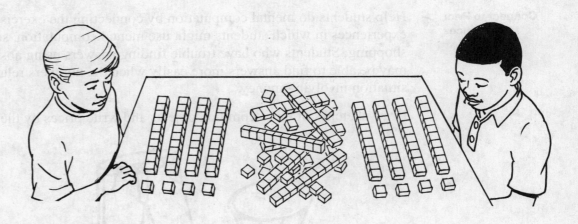

Use Manipulatives ➤ Write 4 × 11, 2 × 13, and 3 × 14 on the board. For each expression, have students first build an array with their place-value models and then give the product. After each product has been found, invite volunteers to describe how they used an array to find it.

Multiplying Two-Digit and One-Digit Numbers

ACCESS CONTENT

Objective Use the standard algorithm to multiply two-digit numbers by one-digit numbers.

ESL Strategies *Use before* **LEARN**   ⏱ 5 MIN

Use Gestures ➤ Write the following problem on the board:

$$\begin{array}{r} 24 \\ \times\, 3 \\ \hline \end{array}$$

Show how to solve the problem using partial products. As you say and write each step on the board, point to the digits and numbers you are using. **We can multiply 24 × 3 using partial products. First we can break 24 into ones and tens. How many ones are in 24?** *(4 ones)* **How many tens are in 24?** *(2 tens)* **What number is 2 tens?** *(20)* **What is the product of 3 × 4?** *(12)* **That's right. The first partial product is 12. What is the product of 3 × 20?** *(60)* **Yes. The second partial product is 60. To find the final product, what do we do?** *(Find the sum of the partial products.)* **What is that sum?** *(12 + 60 = 72)*

$$\begin{array}{r} 24 \\ \times\, 3 \\ \hline \end{array}
\qquad
\begin{array}{lcl}
3 \times 4 & = & 12 \leftarrow \text{first partial product} \\
3 \times 20 & = & 60 \leftarrow \text{second partial product} \\
\end{array}$$

$$72 \leftarrow \text{final product}$$

Write the following exercises, excluding answers, on the board. Invite volunteers to come to the board and emulate your gestures as they demonstrate how to find the partial products and final products.

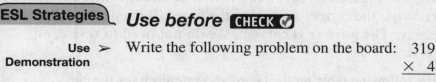

$$\begin{array}{r} 32 \\ \times\, 5 \\ \hline \end{array}
\qquad\qquad
\begin{array}{r} 45 \\ \times\, 4 \\ \hline \end{array}
\qquad\qquad
\begin{array}{r} 29 \\ \times\, 4 \\ \hline \end{array}$$

$$\quad (160) \qquad\qquad\qquad (180) \qquad\qquad\qquad (87)$$

Multiplying Three-Digit and One-Digit Numbers

ACCESS CONTENT; EXTEND LANGUAGE

Objective Use the standard algorithm to multiply three-digit numbers by one-digit numbers.

ESL Strategies *Use before* **CHECK ✓**   ⏱ 5–10 MIN

Use ➤ Write the following problem on the board:
Demonstration

$$\begin{array}{r} 319 \\ \times\; 4 \\ \hline \end{array}$$

Work step-by-step with students to find the product using the standard algorithm. Write all the computations on the board. **Multiply the ones.**

(4 × 9 ones = 36 ones) **Regroup any tens.** *(36 ones = 3 tens, 6 ones)*
Multiply the tens. *(4 × 1 = 4 tens)* **Add the regrouped tens.** *(4 tens +
3 tens = 7 tens)* **Multiply the hundreds.** *(4 × 3 hundreds = 12 hundreds)*
What is the place value of the digit 1? *(One thousands place)* **Regroup
any thousands.** *(12 hundreds = 1 thousand, 2 hundreds)* **What is the
product?** *(1,276)*

Point to 319 and ask: **How many hundreds are there in this number?** *(3)*
Write 300 on the board. Repeat for tens *(1)* and ones *(9)*. Then work with
students to find the following products. Write all the computation on the board.

$$
\begin{array}{ccc}
300 & 10 & 9 \\
\times\ 4 & \times\ 4 & \times\ 4 \\
\hline
(1{,}200) & (40) & (36)
\end{array}
$$

Ask a volunteer to add the 3 partial products. *(1,200 + 40 + 36 = 1,276)*

**Have Students ➤
Report Back
Orally**

Have student pairs copy all the computation from the board onto a sheet of
paper and keep it at their desks for reference. Write the words "multiply,"
"regroup," "partial product," and "sum" on the board. Then have the pairs
divide a sheet of paper into 2 halves with a pencil line. Invite them to use the
words on the board to list the steps of the standard algorithm and then to list
the steps for using partial products. Have them tell what is different about the
2 methods of finding the product of 319 × 4 and what is the same.

Problem-Solving Strategy:
Try, Check, and Revise

USE WITH LESSON

5-7

EXTEND LANGUAGE

Objective Solve problems using the *Try, Check, and Revise* strategy.

ESL Strategies   *Use before*   **LEARN**   ⏱ 5 MIN

Focus on Meaning ➤

Write the following on the board.

Jack is taller than Bill. Sue is shorter than Jack but taller than Bill.
Jack is shorter than Alan. Who is the tallest?

Try to guess the answer. Think about a reasonable choice. Have a
volunteer make a guess. Write it on the board. **Check to see if the guess
written on the board is the correct answer or not.** Draw a picture on the
board to show the height relationships among the four people. If the name
on the board is incorrect, say: **Let's revise, or change, this answer so it is
correct.** Write the correct answer on the board. If the name on the board is
correct, say: **The answer is correct. We do not need to revise, or
change, it.**

Draw the following table on the board as a reference for the class.

Try	Take a guess.
Check	See if your guess is correct.
Revise	Take another guess if the first guess was not correct.

Choose a Computation Method

USE WITH LESSON 5-8

ACCESS CONTENT

Objective For a variety of problems, state the computation method to be used and multiply using that method.

Materials *(per student)* Drawing paper; crayons or felt pens

ESL Strategies   *Use before* **CHECK** ✓   ⏲ 15–20 MIN

Paraphrase Ideas ➤ **There are 3 methods, or ways, to solve a multiplication problem.** On the board, write the column headings "Mental Math," "Paper and Pencil," and "Calculator." **When would you use mental math?** *(When the problem is easy to do in your head)* Write "easy to do in your head" under "Mental Math." **When would you use paper and pencil?** *(When you need to regroup only once or twice)* Write "not a lot of regroupings" under "Paper and Pencil." **When would you use a calculator?** *(When there are a lot of regroupings)* Write "many regroupings" under "Calculator."

Use Graphic ➤ Have students work in groups to make posters that show when to use each
Organizers   computation method. Have them include a multiplication expression under each heading, for example: 2 × 203 under "Mental Math," 281 × 3 under "Paper and Pencil," and 3,472 × 4 under "Calculator."

Multiplying Money

USE WITH LESSON 5-9

ACCESS CONTENT

Objective Calculate products involving amounts of money.

Materials *(per group)* Bill and Coin Models (Teaching Tool 7) or play money: 5 one-dollar bills, 21 dimes, 15 pennies

ESL Strategies   *Use before* **LEARN**   ⏲ 10–15 MIN

Use Manipulatives ➤ Write $1.75 on the board. Then write $1.00 + 70¢ + 5¢. This is another way to write $1.75. How many pennies are in 5¢? *(5)* How many dimes are in 70¢? *(7)* How many dollar bills are in $1.00? *(1)*

Assign students to groups, and give each group a supply of play money. **If a postcard at the museum costs $1.75, how much do 3 postcards cost?** Have students count out $1.75 for each postcard: 3 dollars, 21 dimes, and 15 pennies. Then have students trade their dimes for dollars and their pennies for dimes. **How much money do you have altogether?** (*5 dollar bills, 2 dimes, and 5 pennies, or $5.25*)

You can also multiply to find the answer. Write the following on the board:

$1.75 per postcard
×   3 postcards

You multiply just as you would if the dollar sign and the decimal point weren't there. Work through the multiplication algorithm with students to find the product $5.25.

Multiplying Three Factors

USE WITH LESSON
5-10

ACCESS CONTENT

Objective Use the Commutative and Associative Properties to simplify multiplication with three factors.

ESL Strategies

Use Small-Group Interactions

Use before **CHECK** ✓   ⏱ 10 MIN

Assign students to groups. Write $3 \times 4 = 12$ on the board. Ask each group to find the other way to write this multiplication sentence. (*4 × 3 = 12*) **You can multiply the 2 numbers in either order. Does the product change?** (*No*)

Write $2 \times 7 = 14$ and $3 \times 9 = 27$ on the board. Ask each group to decide on the other way to write each sentence. (*7 × 2 = 14; 9 × 3 = 27*)

Then write $(5 \times 7) \times 2 = 70$. Ask each group to find the other way to group the factors in this multiplication sentence. (*5 × (7 × 2) = 70*) **Does changing the grouping of the factors change the product?** (*No*)

Write $4 \times (2 \times 3) = 24$ and $(5 \times 1) \times 6 = 30$ on the board. Ask each group to decide on the other way to group the factors for each multiplication sentence. (*(4 × 2) × 3 = 24; 5 × (1 × 6) = 30*)

Problem-Solving Skill: Choose an Operation

ACCESS CONTENT

Objective Identify the appropriate operation needed to solve a problem.

Materials *(per group)* 4 index cards, each marked with one of the operation symbols: $+$, $-$, $\times$, $\div$.

ESL Strategies   *Use before* **LEARN**   🕐 5 MIN

Use Total ➤
Physical Response

Remind students that an expression is at least 2 numbers joined by an operation symbol. Write $14 + 67$ on the board. **Is this an expression?** *(Yes)* Write $\$1.00 = 4$ quarters on the board. **Is this an expression?** *(No)* Distribute the operation symbol cards. Then write 60 __ 3 on the board, and read the following problem: **If there are 60 seconds in 1 minute, how many seconds are there in 3 minutes?** Have students in each group decide which operation symbol they would use to complete the expression and solve the problem. Have them hold up the card showing that symbol. Ask a volunteer from each group to explain his or her choice. Then write $\times$ in the blank. **Does 60×3 show how to find the number of seconds in 3 minutes?** *(Yes)* Repeat the procedure with the following problems.

Write 275 __ 229 on the board. **Stella has 275 stickers. Mia has 229 stickers. How many more stickers does Stella have than Mia?** *(− ; 46)*

Write 63 __ 9 on the board. **Ramon has 63 stamps. He put 9 stamps on each page of his stamp album. How many pages did Ramon use?** *(÷ ; 7)*

Write 1,024 __ 2,739 on the board. **There are 1,024 pennies in one pile and 2,739 pennies in another pile. How many pennies are there altogether?** *(+ ; 3,763)*

Problem-Solving Applications: Jumbo Jet

ACCESS CONTENT

Objective Review and apply key concepts, skills, and strategies learned in this and previous chapters.

Materials *(per student)* Calculator

ESL Strategies   *Use before* **LEARN**   🕐 5 MIN

Use Small-Group ➤
Interactions

Read aloud the following word problem, excluding the answer, and then write it on the board.

> Mr. Jones drives at a rate of 35 miles per hour. How far could he travel in 3 hours at this rate? *(105 miles)*

Have students work in groups, using their calculators to help them solve the problem. Encourage students to ask each other questions such as, "What multiplication sentence can we use to solve the problem?" and "What key should you press to show multiplication?" and "What does the display show?"

Multiplying by Multiples of Ten

EXTEND LANGUAGE

Objective Multiply mentally any two-digit number by a multiple of 10, 100, or 1,000.

ESL Strategies

Have Students Create Test Items ➤

Use before CHECK ✓

⏱ 10–15 MIN

Remind students that it is often easier to multiply numbers in our head if the factors are multiples of 10. Then divide the class into groups. Have each group write 5 multiplication expressions on a sheet of paper. One factor of each expression should be a 2-digit multiple of 10 (i.e., 10 through 90). The other factor should be a 4-digit multiple of 1,000 (i.e., 1,000 through 9,000).

Have groups exchange papers. At your signal, each group solves the problems. When all the teams have finished, students review their answers and calculate their scores. Each team gets 1 point for each correct answer. In addition, the team that finishes first gets 1 extra point.

Estimating Products

ACCESS CONTENT

Objective Use rounding and place value to estimate products of larger numbers.

Vocabulary Rounding

ESL Strategies

Use before LEARN

⏱ 5–10 MIN

Give Frequent Feedback ➤

Remind students that they can round factors to the nearest tens value to estimate, or guess, the product. Write $17 \times 39 = \_\_$ on the board. Let's estimate the product using <u>rounding</u>. How many digits does each factor have? *(2)* So what place value should we round each number to? *(The nearest tens)* Which digit do we look at to round to the nearest tens? *(The ones digit)* What number should we round 17 to? *(20)* What number should we round 39 to? *(40)* So how should we estimate the product of 17 × 39? *(20 × 40 = 800)* Then write 721 × 67 = __ on the board. Invite students to tell you how to find a range of products. Remind students that the range tells the least and greatest estimates of the product. Follow students' instructions for finding the range. *(700 × 60 = 42,000; 800 × 70 = 56,000; the product is between 42,000 and 56,000.)*

Using Arrays to Multiply

USE WITH LESSON 6-3

EXTEND LANGUAGE

Objective Use arrays to find products involving two-digit factors.

Vocabulary Partial products

ESL Strategies **Use before** **LEARN** ⏱ 5 MIN

Focus on Meaning ➤ Use the everyday meaning of *partial* to remind students of the mathematical meaning of <u>partial products</u>. **If we make a list of all the students in our class, that would be a list of *part* of all the students in the whole school. This means we would have a *partial* list of all the students in our school.** Then provide an example of multiplication using partial products. Write 11 × 7 = (10 × 7) + (1 × 7) on the board.

Explain each step as you write on the board.

10 × 7 = 70 **70 is a *partial product*. It is *part* of the product of 11 × 7.**

1 × 7 = 7 **7 is a *partial product*. It is part of the product of 11 × 7.**

70 + 7 = 77 **To find the whole product, add the partial products.**

Problem-Solving Strategy: Make an Organized List

USE WITH LESSON 6-4

ACCESS CONTENT

Objective Make an organized list to represent information given in a problem.

Materials 3 different colored markers; pen; pencil

Use before LEARN

⏱ 10–15 MIN

Use Real Objects ➤ Display the 3 markers. Then display the pencil and pen. (Substitute available materials for suggested ones, as long as you have 3 of one type of item and 2 of another.) Explain to students that one way to solve a problem is to make an organized list of all the different possible combinations of the parts involved in the problem. **Suppose that we want to draw a picture using only 1 colored marker and either a pencil or a pen. We can make a list to show all the possible combinations that we have to choose from.**

Invite a volunteer to come to the front and to choose 1 colored marker and either the pencil or the pen. Write the combination on the board (e.g., "blue marker, pencil"). Have the student keep the marker but exchange the pencil for the pen. Write this combination on the board beneath the first ("blue marker, pen"). Have the student replace the pen and take the marker back to his or her seat. Have a second volunteer come forward and choose one of the remaining markers and either the pencil or the pen. Write the new combination on the board (e.g., "orange marker, pen"). Have the student keep the marker but exchange the pen for the pencil. Write that combination ("orange marker, pencil"). Have the student replace the pencil and take the marker back to his or her seat. Ask a third volunteer to come forward and combine the last marker with the pencil and pen in turn. Write these combinations on the board. Point to the list of combinations. **How many combinations did we list?** *(6)* **Are those all the different combinations?** *(Yes)*

Multiplying by Two-Digit Numbers

USE WITH LESSON
6-5

ACCESS CONTENT

Objectives Use the partial products and the standard algorithm for multiplying with two-digit factors.

Materials *(per group)* $\frac{1}{4}$-Inch Grid Paper (Teaching Tool 4); scissors

Use before LEARN

⏱ 10 MIN

Use ➤
Demonstration Demonstrate how to form a 31 × 22 array on grid paper by outlining and then cutting out an area comprising 31 rows and 22 columns. **There are 22 squares in a row and there are 31 rows. So there are 31 groups. How many squares are in each group? We can multiply the number of rows by the number of columns.** Write 31 × 22 = __ on the board. **I can use partial products to multiply 31 × 22.**

Cut off one row of 22 squares and hold up the 22 × 30 array. **If I cut off one row of squares, how many rows of 22 are in this array?** *(30)* **How can we find the number of squares in the array?** On the board, write 30 × 22 squares = __ squares. **How can we break apart 30 to make it easier to multiply?** *(Break down 30 into 3 tens.)* Write 10 × 3 on the board. **Then we can use properties to help us multiply 30 × 22.** Write 10 × (3 × 22) = 10 × 66 = 660 squares.

Hold up the 1 × 22 array. **How many squares are in this array?** *(22)* **So how many squares were in the 31 × 22 array?** *(660 + 22 = 682 squares)*

Use Manipulatives ➤ Assign students to groups, and give each group grid paper and scissors. On the board, write 14 × 22 = ___ . Have students use their grid paper and scissors to find the product. *(Sample partial arrays include: (10 × 22) + (4 × 22) = 220 + 88 = 308; (14 × 20) + (14 × 2) = 280 + 28 = 308)*

Multiplying Greater Numbers

USE WITH LESSON 6-6

ACTIVATE PRIOR KNOWLEDGE/BUILD BACKGROUND

Objective Use the standard algorithm to multiply two-digit numbers by three- or four-digit numbers.

Materials Colored chalk

ESL Strategies **Use before** **LEARN** 🕐 5 MIN

Connect to Prior ➤ **You already know the steps for multiplying by a two-digit number.**
Knowledge of
Math Write the following problem on the board.
$$\begin{array}{r} 37 \\ \times\, 25 \\ \hline \end{array}$$

Have volunteers come up to the board one at a time. Have the first volunteer describe the first step of the algorithm. **What is the first step we must do to solve this problem?** *(5 × 7 ones = 35 ones)* Have the student use colored chalk to show that step. **How did you show the 35 ones?** *(I wrote 5 in the ones place of the product. I regrouped the 30 ones as 3 tens. I then wrote the regrouped 3 tens above the 3 in the problem.)* Have different volunteers show the subsequent steps of the algorithm in the same way. Each student should use a different color chalk to show his or her step.

Repeat with the following problem.
$$\begin{array}{r} 3{,}194 \\ \times\quad 28 \\ \hline \end{array}$$
(89,432)

Choose a Computation Method

USE WITH LESSON 6-7

ACCESS CONTENT

Objective Decide on an appropriate computational method to use to find a product.

Materials *(per student)* Calculator

ESL Strategies **Use before** **LEARN** 🕐 10 MIN

Use Pantomime ➤ Introduce 3 pantomime gestures. **This means mental math:** Tap your head. **This means paper and pencil:** Pantomime writing by moving your wrist. **And this means calculator.** Press with your index finger several times on your palm as if on calculator keys. Write 12 × 453 = __ on the board. Then point to the number sentence and say: **Which computation method should I use?** Then use the pantomime gestures in any order as students say "Yes," or "No." **That's right. Paper and pencil is the best method here. Why?** *(Because you don't have to regroup too often)*

Write the following number sentences, excluding answers, on the board.

10 × $300 = *(Mental math: $3,000)*

39 × $267 = *(Calculator: $10,413)*

11 × $220 = *(Paper and pencil: $2,420)*

Point to each number sentence, and ask students to pantomime the best computation method for it. Ask them to tell why they chose that method. Finally, have them use that method to find the product.

Multiplying Money

ACCESS CONTENT

USE WITH LESSON 6-8

Objective Compute and estimate products involving money amounts.

Materials *(per student)* Bill and coin models (Teaching Tool 7) or play money: 50 pennies, 50 dimes, 50 $1 bills

ESL Strategies **Use before** **LEARN**   🕐 15 MIN

Use Manipulatives ➤ Write the following exercises, excluding answers, on the board.

$3.12	$1.11	$2.43
× 22	× 13	× 12
($64.84)	($14.83)	($29.16)

Write the words "penny," "dime," and "dollar" on the board. Read each word aloud together with the students. As you point to each, have them identify the rightmost digit in each multiplication problem as the number of pennies, the middle digit as the number of dimes, and the leftmost digit as the number of dollar bills.

Then have students use play money to find each product, modeling one step of the algorithm at a time and trading for larger denominations when possible.

1 dollar   1 dime   1 penny

Problem-Solving Skill: Writing to Explain

USE WITH LESSON 6-9

Objective Write to explain a pattern.

ESL Strategies

Use before **LEARN**

⏱ 10 MIN

Have Students ➤ Report Back Orally

Draw the following pictograph on the board.

How many stamps does Marla have? We can write down the steps we need to help us solve the problem. Write the following steps on the board. Have volunteers write in the answers.

1. Each picture stands for *(10)* stamps.

2. The pictograph shows *(8)* pictures for Marla.

3. Multiply 10 *(stamps)* × 8 *(pictures)*. Marla has *(80 stamps)*.

Group students in pairs. Place English language learners with students who are fluent in English. Have one partner write the steps to find the number of stamps that Rashid has and the other partner write the steps to find the number of stamps that Karen has. Have students exchange papers and use their partners' steps to find the answers.

Problem-Solving Applications: Reptiles

USE WITH LESSON 6-10

Objective Review and apply key concepts, skills, and strategies learned in this and previous chapters.

Materials *(per group)* Centimeter ruler or meter stick; piece of string 150 centimeters long; scissors

ESL Strategies

Use before **LEARN**

⏱ 10 MIN

Use Small-Group ➤ Interactions

Read aloud the following word problem, excluding the answer, and then write it on the board.

The line John drew is 10 times longer than the line Sally drew. If Sally's line is 12 centimeters long, how long is John's line? *(120 centimeters)*

Have students work in groups, using the string and ruler to help them solve the problem. Students should first measure and cut off a piece of string 12 centimeters long. Then they should use that length to mark off 10 such lengths on the remaining piece, cutting the string at the end of the tenth length. Finally, they should measure the length of that piece.

Using Patterns to Divide Mentally

ACCESS CONTENT

USE WITH LESSON
7-1

Objective Divide multiples of 10, 100, and 1,000 by a one-digit number.

Materials *(per group)* 2 copies of Centimeter Grid Paper (Teaching Tool 6)

ESL Strategies

Use before **LEARN**

⏱ 10–15 MIN

Use Small-Group Interactions

Assign students to groups and give each group grid paper. Have students outline a box that contains 80 squares. Then model the following activity.

I want to divide my 80-square box into 4 equal parts. What expression shows how many squares will be in each part of my box? *(80 ÷ 4)* Write 80 ÷ 4 = __ on the board. Show students how to count out squares, and then draw horizontal and vertical lines that will divide the box into 4 groups of 20 squares each. **How many squares are there in each part?** *(20)* **You can also find 80 ÷ 4 by thinking of a simple division fact: 8 ÷ 4 = 2. How would you use this division fact to find the answer?** *(8 tens ÷ 4 = 2 tens, or 20. So there are 20 squares in each part.)*

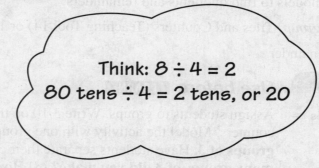

Think: 8 ÷ 4 = 2
80 tens ÷ 4 = 2 tens, or 20

Repeat the activity by asking students to identify the number of squares in each of 8 equal groups. (8 ÷ 8 = 1, so 80 ÷ 8 is the same as 8 tens ÷ 8 = 1 ten, or 10.) Have students use grid paper to confirm the number of squares in each of the 8 equal parts. Continue with 80 ÷ 2 and 80 ÷ 10. Then have students outline a box containing 200 squares. Ask them to find the number of squares in each part for the divisors 4, 5, and 10. Ask a volunteer to write the division sentence for each on the board.

Estimating Quotients

ACCESS CONTENT

USE WITH LESSON
7-2

Objective Estimate quotients.

Vocabulary Compatible numbers, overestimate, underestimate

Use before **CHECK ✓**   ⏲ 10–15 MIN

Use Graphic ➤
Organizers

Write the following headings on the board: "Term," "Meaning," and "Example."

Beneath "Term," write "compatible numbers." **What are compatible numbers?** *(Numbers that are easy to work with in your head)* Write the definition in the second column. In the third column write 257 ÷ 5 = ___ and 250 ÷ 5 = 50.

Have students copy the information from the board to add to a Math Terms Dictionary. Then write the terms overestimate and underestimate on the board. Ask students to repeat each word after you. **What is an overestimate?** *(An estimate that is higher than the exact answer)* **What is an underestimate?** *(An estimate that is lower than the exact answer)* **Is 50 an overestimate or an underestimate for 257 ÷ 5?** *(An underestimate)* Invite students to add these terms to their dictionaries and to show examples using division in the third column.

Dividing with Remainders

USE WITH LESSON
7-3

ACCESS CONTENT

Objective Use models to find quotients and remainders.

Materials *(per group)* Tiles and Counters (Teaching Tool 14) or 12 counters

Vocabulary Remainder

ESL Strategies

Use before **LEARN**   ⏲ 10–15 MIN

Use Manipulatives ➤

Assign students to groups. Write 3)‾10 on the board, and give each group 10 counters. Model the activity with one group. **Divide your 10 counters into groups of 3.** Have students separate their counters into groups of 3. **How many groups of 3 did you make?** *(3)* **How many counters are in each group?** *(3)* Point to each group as you count aloud. **What was the total number of counters you were able to place evenly into groups of 3?** *(9)* **Are there any counters left over?** *(Yes)* **How many?** *(1)* Complete the algorithm on the board:

$$\begin{array}{r} 3 \\ 3\overline{)10} \\ -9 \\ \hline 1 \end{array}$$

The amount left over in a division problem is called the remainder. Point to the 1 counter not in a group of 3, and then point to the 1 in the algorithm. **This remainder is the number of counters that could not be used in a group of 3. We write this quotient as 3 R1. What does the letter _R_ stand for?** *(Remainder)*

Give each group 2 more counters, and repeat the activity with $12 \div 5$. *(2 R2)*

Two-Digit Quotients

EXTEND LANGUAGE

USE WITH LESSON 7-4

Objective Use models and the standard algorithm to divide 2-digit numbers by 1-digit numbers.

Materials *(per pair)* Place-Value Blocks, Set 1 (Teaching Tool 2) or 5 tens models and 20 ones models

ESL Strategies

Have Students ➤
Report Back
Orally

Use before CHECK ✓

10–15 MIN

Write the following problem on the board.

> Chang has 34 marbles and 4 empty bags. He wants to put the same number of marbles in each bag. How many marbles can he put in each bag?

Have students model the problem in pairs. Give each pair 5 tens models and 20 ones models. Call on students to report back orally on how they solved the problem. Invite them to describe the way in which they modeled regrouping the tens and how they determined what the remainder is. *(Sample answer: Since there are no tens in the answer, I regrouped 3 tens models as 30 ones, and added 4 ones. Then I divided the 34 ones into 4 groups of 8, plus 2 extra ones. The answer is 8 marbles, with 2 left over, or 8 R2.)*

Dividing Two-Digit Numbers

ACCESS CONTENT

USE WITH LESSON 7-5

Objective Use a standard algorithm to divide a two-digit number by a one-digit number.

Materials *(per pair)* Place-Value Blocks, Set 1 (Teaching Tool 2) or 5 tens models and 20 ones models

Vocabulary Dividend, divisor, quotient

ESL Strategies

Use Small-Group ➤
Interactions

Use before LEARN

5 MIN

Assign students to groups and give each group a set of place-value blocks. Write the following problem on the board. Read the problem together with students.

> Selma has 42 books. She wants to put them on 3 shelves, and she wants to put the same number of books on each shelf. How many books can she put on each shelf?

Use Manipulatives ➤ **What is the <u>dividend</u> in this problem?** *(42)* Write 42 on the board. **What is the <u>divisor</u>?** *(3)* Write 3)42 on the board.

Have students show 42 with their place-value models. Then have them separate the 4 tens into 3 equal groups. **How many tens does each group get?** *(1)* On the board, write 1 in the tens place of the <u>quotient</u>. **How many tens have been used?** *(3)* Point to the numbers as you say: **3 times 1 equals?** *(3)* Pause for students to answer, then write -3 in the algorithm. **How many tens are left over?** *(1)* Point to the numbers as you say: **4 minus 3 equals?** *(1)* Write 1 under -3. **How many ones do you have?** *(2)* Write 2 next to the 1. Tell students to trade their last ten block for 10 ones. Then have them divide their 12 ones into 3 equal groups and continue through the rest of the algorithm. **What is the answer to the problem?** *(Selma can put 14 books on each of 3 shelves.)*

$$\begin{array}{r} 14 \\ 3\overline{)42} \\ -3 \\ \hline 12 \\ -12 \\ \hline 0 \end{array}$$

Pat can put 14 books on each shelf.

Problem-Solving Skill: Interpreting Remainders

ACCESS CONTENT

Objective Decide how to use the quotient and remainder to answer the question in a division problem.

Materials *(per student)* Drawing paper and crayons

ESL Strategies | *Use before* **LEARN** | ⏱ 5–10 MIN

Use Pictures ➤ Pass out paper and crayons. Explain that when you buy batteries at the store, they often come in packages of 2. Have students draw a picture of a package with 2 batteries in it. Read the following problem and then write it on the board. If necessary, show students a battery or draw a picture of a battery on the board. **I need 9 batteries for my radio. The batteries are sold in packages of 2. How many packages must I buy?**

Have students combine their battery pictures to arrive at an answer. **How many packages must I buy?** *(5)* **How many batteries will I have?** *(10)* **How many batteries will I have left over?** *(1)*

Write $9 \div 2 = 4\,R1$ on the board. Why do you have to buy more batteries than you need? *(Since each package has 2 batteries, 4 packages have only 8 batteries in all. Therefore, you have to buy another package to get the 9 batteries you need.)*

Dividing Three-Digit Numbers

USE WITH LESSON 7-7

EXTEND LANGUAGE

Objective Use the standard algorithm to divide 3-digit numbers by 1-digit numbers.

Materials *(per student)* Index cards marked "estimate," "more than," "less than," and "close to"

ESL Strategies | *Use before* **LEARN**

 5–10 MIN

Focus on Meaning ➤ Write the following words and phrases on the board: "estimate," "more than," "less than," and "close to." Invite students to repeat the words after you.

Explain that knowing the meaning of these words helps us decide where to start writing the quotient in a division problem.

Write on the board the following sentences, excluding answers. As you read each statement aloud, have students hold up the card with the word or phrase that will correctly complete the statement.

> **When we find about how many groups a number can be divided into, we __ the quotient.** *(Estimate)*

> **When we estimate a quotient, we can use a compatible number that is __ the dividend.** *(Close to)*

> **If we use a compatible number that is __ the actual dividend, our estimate will be a little too high.** *(More than)*

> **If we use a compatible number that is __ the actual dividend, our estimate will be a little too low.** *(Less than)*

Zeros in the Quotient

ACCESS CONTENT

USE WITH LESSON 7-8

Objective Divide with zeros in the quotient.

Materials *(per group)* Place-Value Blocks, Set 1 (Teaching Tool 2) or 5 tens models and 10 ones models

ESL Strategies *Use before* **LEARN** 🕐 5–10 MIN

Use Manipulatives ➤ Assign students to groups, and give each group place-value blocks. Write the following problem on the board.

$$2\overline{)21}$$

Have students model 21. **If I divide the tens into 2 groups, how many tens will each group have?** *(1 ten)* Have students show this as you write 1 in the tens place of the quotient on the board. **How many ones do you have?** *(1)* **There are not enough ones to divide into 2 groups. What should I do?** *(Write a zero in the ones place of the quotient.)* Write 0 in the quotient. Then write R1 as you say: **What is the remainder?** *(1)*

Write the following problem on the board.

$$3\overline{)32}$$

Have students use the place-value blocks to model the problem. Invite a volunteer to complete the problem on the board.

Dividing Money Amounts

ACTIVATE PRIOR KNOWLEDGE/BUILD BACKGROUND

Objective Compute and estimate quotients involving money amounts.

ESL Strategies | *Use before* CHECK ✓ | 🕐 5–10 MIN

Use Role Playing ➤ Draw the following multi-packs of items on the board.

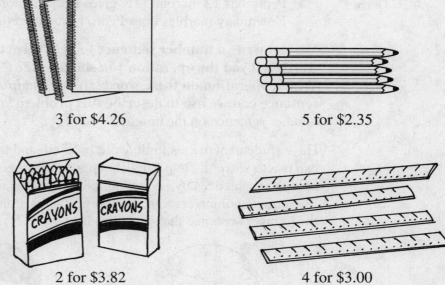

3 for $4.26   5 for $2.35

2 for $3.82   4 for $3.00

Have pairs of students role-play shopping in a store. One student plays the role of a shopper and the other student plays the role of a salesperson. The shopper points to an item, says that he or she wants to know the price of just 1 of the items, and writes a division sentence for the problem. For example, to show buying 1 pencil, the shopper would write $2.35 ÷ 5 = _____. The salesperson must tell what the cost is and explain how to find the answer. For example, to find $2.35 ÷ 5: I divide the way I would with whole numbers. 235 ÷ 5 = 47. Then I show the dollar sign and decimal point in the quotient. If the quotient is less than 1 dollar, I write 0 before the decimal point. $2.35 ÷ 5 = $0.47. One pencil costs $0.47. Students should switch roles so that each plays both roles twice. Guide the activity as necessary. If students have trouble articulating an answer, ask questions that include key words to prompt the correct response.

Problem-Solving Strategy: Write a Number Sentence

EXTEND LANGUAGE

Objective Write number sentences for word problems, and use complete sentences to write answers to word problems.

ESL Strategies

> Have Students
> Report Back
> Orally

Use before **LEARN**

🕐 10–15 MIN

Write the following problem on the board.

> Pedro has 12 marbles. Tia gives Pedro 9 more marbles. How many marbles does Pedro have altogether?

We can write a number sentence to help solve this word problem. Which words tell you the operation you should use? *("More" and "altogether")* **Which operation do these words show?** *(Addition)* **What number sentence can we use to describe this problem?** *(12 + 9 = 21)* Write the number sentence on the board.

Have students write a simple word problem and the number sentence they can use to solve it. Help English language learners articulate their ideas into complete sentences by reviewing their problems for spelling and grammar. Then invite volunteers to read their problems aloud and tell how they wrote the number sentence that describes it.

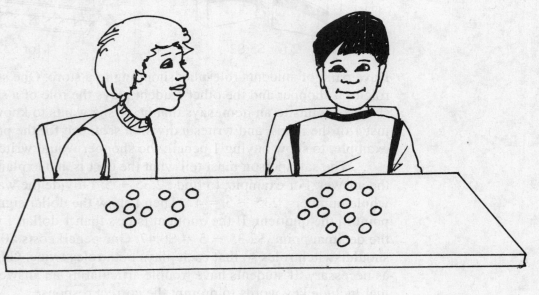

Divisibility Rules

ACCESS CONTENT

Objective Determine mentally if a number is divisible by 2, 3, 5, 9, or 10.

Materials *(per student)* Calculator

Vocabulary Divisible, divisibility rules

ESL Strategies

Use before CHECK ✓

🕐 5–10 MIN

Use Graphic Organizers ➤ **A number is divisible by another number if the quotient has no remainder.** Write the following headings on the board: "Divisible By," "Rule," and "Example." Under "Divisible By," write 2. **How can you tell if a whole number is divisible by 2?** *(If the ones digit is an even number: 0, 2, 4, 6, 8)* Write the divisibility rule in the second column. **What are some numbers that are divisible by 2?** *(Accept any answers that have an even number in the ones place and write them in the third column.)*

Have students use their calculators to check the answers on the board. For example, if 26 is suggested as a number that is divisible by 2, students would press "2, 6, division symbol, 2," and the "equal/enter" key. **The display on your calculator shows an answer of 13.** Explain that the answer is a whole number. So, the example is correct. **If the quotient has numbers to the right of a decimal point, then it is not a whole number. So, the dividend is not divisible by 2.**

Use Peer Questioning ➤ Have students copy the headings from the board to add to a Math Terms Dictionary. Write 3, 5, 9, and 10 in the first column. Then have pairs of students complete the table by writing the divisibility rules and some examples for each. Encourage students to check the dividends with their calculators and to ask their partners questions such as, "Why is that number divisible by 3?" and "Why isn't that number divisible by 5?"

Finding Averages

EXTEND LANGUAGE

Objective Find the average (mean) of a set of numbers.

Vocabulary Average

ESL Strategies | *Use before* **LEARN** | ⏱ 10–15 MIN

Use ➤ Write the following steps on the board. **Look at these steps. Read each step**
Demonstration **together with me.**

> Step 1: Add the numbers.
> Step 2: Divide the sum by the number of numbers.

You use these steps to find an <u>average</u>. Write $2 + 3 + 4$ on the board. **Step**
1 says to add the numbers. So, I add 2 plus 3 plus 4. What is the sum?
(9) **Step 2 says to divide the sum by the number of numbers. What is 9**
divided by 3? *(3)* **What is the average of 2, 3, and 4?** *(3)*

Repeat the procedure with 4, 6, 6, and 8. *(Step 1: 4 + 6 + 6 + 8 = 24;*
Step 2: 24 ÷ 4 = 6. The average of 4, 6, 6, and 8 is 6.) Invite a volunteer to
tell the class how to work through each step.

Use Small-Group ➤ Organize the students into small groups. Ask the students to come up with
Interactions some lists of numbers for which to find averages. Have each group work
through the steps on the board. Then invite volunteers from the groups to
share one of their lists of numbers with the class and explain how they found
the average.

Dividing by Multiples of 10

ACCESS CONTENT

Objective Divide multiples of 10, 100, and 1,000 by multiples of 10.

Materials Calculator

ESL Strategies | *Use before* **LEARN** | ⏱ 10–15 MIN

Use Gestures ➤ Write the following equations, excluding answers, on the board.

$$8 \div 4 \qquad = (2)$$
$$80 \div 4 \qquad = (20)$$
$$80 \div 40 \qquad = (2)$$
$$800 \div 40 \qquad = (20)$$

Have a student use a calculator to find the missing quotients. Write the
quotients on the board. One at a time, cross out the zeros on each side of the
last three equations. **What do you see in each equation when I cross out**
the zeros? *(8 ÷ 4 = 2)* Then, for each equation, use your index finger to

show counting the zeros in the dividend, in the divisor, and then in the quotient. **What do you notice about the number of zeros in the dividend and the number of zeros in the divisor? How can it help you find the quotient?** *(You can cross off the same number of zeros from both the dividend and the divisor to find the quotient mentally.)*

Repeat the process with these equations:

$$25 \div 5 \qquad = (5)$$
$$250 \div 5 \qquad = (50)$$
$$250 \div 50 \qquad = (5)$$
$$2,500 \div 50 \qquad = (50)$$

Dividing with Two-Digit Divisors

EXTEND LANGUAGE

USE WITH LESSON 7-14

Objective Estimate quotients with two-digit divisors, and use models to find quotients.

Materials Index cards marked with numbers between 1 and 100

ESL Strategies

Use before **LEARN**

⏱ 5 MIN

Focus on Meaning ➤ **When you compare numbers, you can use words or you can use math symbols**. Write > and < on the board. Point to the greater-than symbol. **What does this symbol mean?** *(Greater than)* Have volunteers say "greater than" statements. Write them on the board first using words and then using the symbol. Repeat this exercise with the less-than symbol.

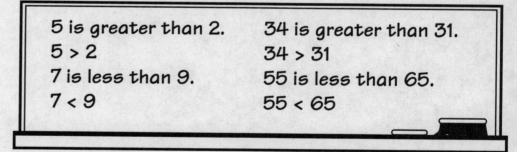

5 is greater than 2.
5 > 2
7 is less than 9.
7 < 9

34 is greater than 31.
34 > 31
55 is less than 65.
55 < 65

Shuffle index cards and divide them into two stacks. Have students choose one card from each stack and say a "greater than" or "less than" statement for the two numbers. Then have them write it in symbols on the board.

Problem-Solving Applications: Equestrian Competitions

ACCESS CONTENT

Objective Review and apply key concepts, skills, and strategies learned in this and previous chapters.

Materials *(per group)* 20 paper clips

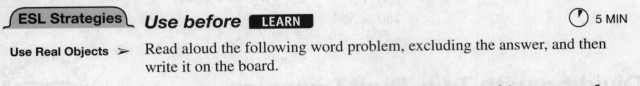

ESL Strategies   *Use before*   **LEARN**   🕐 5 MIN

Use Real Objects ➤ Read aloud the following word problem, excluding the answer, and then write it on the board.

> Ellen and John are playing a game. The winner of the game gets 5 points. So far Ellen has 15 points. How many games has Ellen won? *(3)*

Have groups of students use paper clips to act out the problem. They should show 15 paper clips divided into 3 groups of 5 clips each. Ask volunteers to demonstrate how they solved the problem.

Relating Solids and Plane Figures

ACCESS CONTENT

USE WITH LESSON
8-1

Objective A plane figure has two dimensions: length and width; and a solid figure has three dimensions: length, width, and height.

Materials Power solids; index cards marked "cube," "rectangular prism," "sphere," "cylinder," and "cone"; everyday objects that represent solid figures (ball, food can, funnel, paper cone, rectangular box, cube-shaped block or box, bucket, cylindrical jar)

Vocabulary Solid figure, cube, rectangular prism, sphere, cylinder, cone

ESL Strategies   *Use before*   **LEARN**   🕐 10–15 MIN

Use Real Objects ➤ Assign students to groups. Give each group a different object, such as a ball, can, or funnel. **We are going to be looking at solid figures. Study the object in front of you. Turn it over and around so that you can see it from every direction. Then think of other objects that have the same shape.** Give groups some time with their objects. Then have one member of each group come to the front of the room, display the group's object, and describe it to the class.

Hold up the Power Solid sphere. **What object has a shape like this?** *(The ball)* **An object shaped like this is called a sphere.** Write "sphere" on the board and have students say the word along with you. Ask students to name objects that are shaped like a sphere. *(For example, a globe or a bead)* As students suggest objects, write them on the board below the word "sphere." Then place the sphere and the ball on a table at the front of the room. Place the index card marked "sphere" in front of them.

Repeat the activity with the other objects and models of solid figures. Encourage students to use the words <u>cube</u>, <u>rectangular prism</u>, <u>cylinder</u>, and <u>cone</u>.

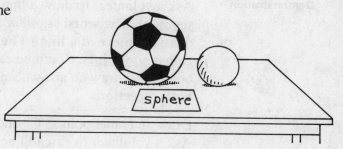

Polygons

EXTEND LANGUAGE

USE WITH LESSON
8-2

Objective Identify and classify polygons.

Materials *(per student)* Ruler; scissors; paper; pencil

Vocabulary Polygon, side, triangle, quadrilateral, pentagon, hexagon, octagon

Focus on Meaning ➤ Write the word "polygon" on the board. Then draw a triangle, a quadrilateral, a pentagon, a hexagon, and an octagon. **These figures are <u>polygons</u>. Their <u>sides</u> are straight. The sides also meet, so the figures are closed.**

Have students draw triangles on their papers and cut them out. Hold up a triangle. Emphasize certain words or syllables as you say: **This polygon is called a <u>triangle</u>.** Invite students to trace the sides with their finger. **How many sides does a triangle have?** *(3)* **How many angles?** *(3)* On the board, write "triangle" and "3 sides" above the triangle.

Have students draw quadrilaterals on their papers and cut them out. Hold up a quadrilateral. Emphasize certain words or syllables as you say: **This polygon is called a <u>quadrilateral</u>.** Invite students to trace the sides with their finger. **How many sides does a quadrilateral have?** *(4)* **How many angles?** *(4)* On the board, write "quadrilateral" and "4 sides" above the quadrilateral. Then repeat the activity for the remaining polygons.

Lines, Line Segments, Rays, and Angles

USE WITH LESSON

8-3

ACCESS CONTENT

Objective Identify important geometric terms relating to lines, parts of a line, and angles.

Vocabulary Point, line, line segment, ray, angle, vertex

Use ➤
Demonstration

Draw and label points "<u>A</u>" and "<u>B</u>" on the board. **A and B are called <u>points</u>.** Ask a volunteer to draw a <u>line</u> connecting them. **(Student) has drawn a <u>line segment.</u> The word *segment* means "piece" or "section." (Student has drawn a piece of a line.) The points at which a line segment ends are called <u>endpoints</u>.** Continue each end of line segment *AB* to the edges of the board, and draw an arrowhead at each edge. **A line continues forever in both directions.**

Draw and label points "<u>C</u>" and "<u>D</u>," and connect them with a line segment. Ask a volunteer to extend line segment <u>CD</u> in one direction to the edge of the board and to draw an arrowhead. **(Student) has drawn a <u>ray</u>. A ray is also part of a line. How many endpoints does a ray have?** *(One)* **A ray continues forever in the other direction.**

Draw rays "*EF*" and "*FG*." **When two rays have the same endpoint, they form an <u>angle</u>. The endpoint that the rays share is called a <u>vertex</u>. What is the vertex of this angle?** *(Point F)* Write "∠*EFG*" and "∠*GFE*" on the board. **We use the points of the rays to name an angle. Where do we always write the vertex?** *(In the middle)*

Have students add the terms *point*, *line*, *line segment*, *endpoint*, *ray*, *angle*, and *vertex* to their math dictionaries.

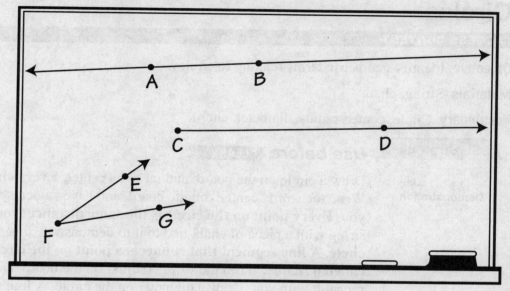

Triangles and Quadrilaterals

USE WITH LESSON 8-4

ACCESS CONTENT

Objective Classify triangles and quadrilaterals.

Materials *(per student)* Geoboard and rubber bands or Dot Paper (Teaching Tool 23)

Vocabulary Equilateral triangle, isosceles triangle, scalene triangle, rectangle, square, trapezoid, parallelogram, rhombus

ESL Strategies

Use before CHECK ✓

⏱ 10–15 MIN

Use Manipulatives ➤ Distribute geoboards or dot paper to students. **Make an <u>equilateral triangle</u>. It can be any size you want.** Invite volunteers to share their work. Have students use language from the lesson to explain why their models or drawings can be classified as equilateral triangles. If students are having trouble articulating their explanation, ask questions to prompt their responses.

Repeat the activity for an <u>isosceles triangle</u>, a <u>scalene triangle</u>, a <u>rectangle</u>, a <u>square</u>, a <u>trapezoid</u>, a <u>parallelogram</u>, and a <u>rhombus</u>.

Circles

ACCESS CONTENT

USE WITH LESSON 8-5

Objective Identify geometric terms relating to circles.

Materials String; chalk

Vocabulary Circle, center, radius, diameter, chord

ESL Strategies | **Use before** | **LEARN** | ⏱ 10 MIN

Use Demonstration ➤ Draw a <u>circle</u> on the board, and mark its <u>center</u>. **Every circle has a center.** Write the word "center" on the board, and have students say it aloud with you. **Every point on the circle is the same distance from the center.** Use a string with a piece of chalk tied to it to demonstrate this. Draw a <u>radius</u> of the circle. **A line segment that connects a point on the circle to the center is called a *radius*.** Write the word "radius" on the board, and have students repeat it with you. Draw a <u>diameter</u> on the circle. **A line segment that connects two points on the circle and passes through the center is called a *diameter*.** Write the word "diameter" on the board, and have students say it aloud with you. Draw a <u>chord</u> on the circle. **A line segment that connects two points on the circle is called a chord.** Write the word "chord" on the board, and have students repeat it with you.

Invite volunteers to come to the board one at a time and draw a circle. Instruct each volunteer to show the center, a radius, a diameter, or a chord on the circle. Correct or confirm each student's response.

Have students add the terms *center, radius, diameter,* and *chord* to their math dictionaries.

Congruent Figures and Motions

ACCESS CONTENT

USE WITH LESSON 8-6

Objective Identify congruent figures, and determine the slide (translation), flip (reflection), or turn (rotation) image of a figure.

Materials *(per group)* 1 paper pattern of a repeated polygon specific to each group; cardboard; pencil; scissors

Vocabulary Congruent

ESL Strategies | **Use before** | **LEARN** | ⏱ 10 MIN

Use Manipulatives ➤ To prepare, draw a paper pattern of a repeated polygon for each group. Each pattern should contain a different repeated polygon.

Assign students to groups. Distribute patterns, cardboard, pencils, and scissors to each group. Tell group members to work together to trace two copies of the polygon onto the cardboard and cut them out. Ask a volunteer to hold up his or her group's two cardboard polygons. **Are these two figures the same size?** *(Yes)* **Are they the same shape?** *(Yes)* **When figures are the same size and the same shape, they are congruent.** Write "congruent" on the board, and have students repeat it with you. Have the volunteer demonstrate congruence by placing one polygon on top of the other. Then have the volunteer hold up one of his or her polygons and one polygon from a neighboring group. **Are these two figures the same size?** *(Answers may vary).* **Are they the same shape?** *(No)* **Are they congruent?** *(No)*

Repeat the activity several more times. Have volunteers hold up two polygons from the same group and say, "These polygons are the same size and have the same shape. They are congruent." Then have other volunteers hold up polygons from two different groups, and say, "These polygons are (not) the same size and do not have the same shape. They are not congruent."

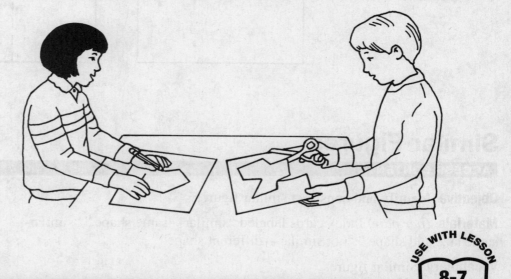

Symmetry

ACCESS CONTENT

Objective Identify and make symmetrical figures, and draw a line or lines of symmetry.

Materials Shapes shown in illustration below; *(per group)* 3 paper shapes that are symmetric; 3 paper shapes that are not symmetric

Vocabulary Symmetric, line of symmetry

ESL Strategies   *Use before* **LEARN**   ⏱ 10 MIN

Use
Demonstration ➤ Cut out the two shapes shown below, and draw the <u>line of symmetry</u> on the first one. Assign students to groups. Hold up the first shape and point to the line of symmetry. **I am going to fold this shape along this line.** Fold it. Unfold the line of symmetry, and point to the congruent parts of the shape on each side of the line. **What can you say about these two parts?** *(They are the same.)* **Point to the line of symmetry. This is the line of symmetry. It is a line that divides a shape into two parts that match or are the same.** Write the phrase "line of symmetry" on the board, and have students say it with you. **If a shape has a line of symmetry, we say that the shape is**

symmetric. Write "symmetric" on the board, and have students say it with you. Hold up the second shape and say that it is *not* symmetric. Ask two volunteers to try folding it into parts that match.

Distribute paper shapes to each group and ask students to decide which are symmetric. When groups are done, hold each shape up one at a time and have the class say, "symmetric" or "not symmetric."

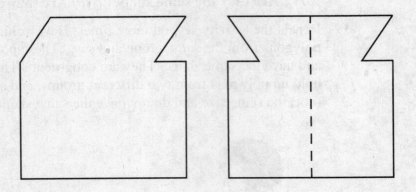

Similar Figures

ACCESS CONTENT

USE WITH LESSON 8-8

Objective Identify and construct similar figures.

Materials *(per pair)* Index cards labeled "similar—same shape," "similar—same size and shape," "not similar—different shape"

Vocabulary Similar figures

ESL Strategies   *Use before* **LEARN**   ⏱ 10 MIN

Use Small-Group Interactions ➤ Assign students to pairs, and model the activity with one pair. Have one partner draw two shapes on a piece of paper. Explain that the two figures can be the same shape or different shapes. They may or may not be the same size. Have the other partner select the index card that describes the figures. Prompt students by saying: **Similar figures have the same shape. Do these figures have the same shape? Are these figures the same size? Which card describes the figures?** *(Students should answer based on shapes as drawn.)* Have partners take turns drawing and classifying pairs of shapes.

Problem-Solving Skill: Writing to Describe

EXTEND LANGUAGE

Objective Describe similarities and differences in geometric figures.

Materials *(per group)* Index card labeled with the name of a geometric figure

ESL Strategies   *Use before* **CHECK** ✓   ◔ 10–15 MIN

Have Students ➤ Report Back in Writing

There are some things you can do to help you write about geometric figures. Write the following list on the board. Then ask volunteers to read the list aloud.

Give each group one index card. Ask students to work together to write brief descriptions of their figures. Encourage students to write complete sentences. Try to pair English language learners with students who are fluent in English. Suggest that students use Lessons 8-1 through 8-5 of their math books to help them review geometric terms.

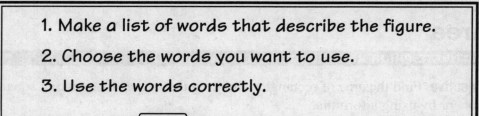

1. Make a list of words that describe the figure.

2. Choose the words you want to use.

3. Use the words correctly.

Perimeter

ACCESS CONTENT

Objective Find the perimeter of a polygon by adding the lengths of the sides or by using a formula.

Materials *(per student)* Geoboard and rubber bands or Dot Paper (Teaching Tool 23)

Vocabulary Perimeter

ESL Strategies   *Use before* **LEARN**   ◔ 10 MIN

Use Manipulatives ➤ Make a unit square on a geoboard as shown.

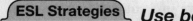

Point to each side of the square and say: **The distance between nails is 1 unit. What is the length of each side?** *(1 unit)* **What is the distance around the square?** *(4 units)* On the board, write $1 + 1 + 1 + 1 = 4$.

Distribute the geoboards. Have students make a square with sides that are each 3 units in length. **How can you find the distance around your square?** *(Add the units on each side.)* Pause as students calculate. **What is the distance around your square?** *(12 units)* **The distance around a polygon is called the <u>perimeter</u>.** Write "perimeter" on the board and have students repeat it with you.

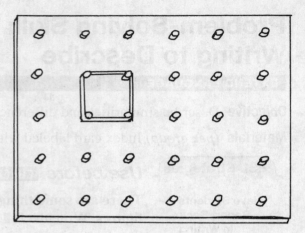

Draw a 1-foot square on the board. Label each side "1 foot." **What is the perimeter of this square?** *(4 feet)* **How do you know?** *(Because 1 foot + 1 foot + 1 foot + 1 foot = 4 feet)* Draw a triangle on the board and label the length of each side in inches. Have students find the perimeter of the triangle. Repeat, using a rectangle marked in centimeters.

Area

USE WITH LESSON 8-11

ACTIVATE PRIOR KNOWLEDGE/BUILD BACKGROUND

Objective Find the area of rectangles and irregular shapes by counting square units or by using a formula.

Materials *(per student)* Centimeter Grid Paper (Teaching Tool 6) or grid paper with large squares; pencil; crayons

Vocabulary Area

ESL Strategies

Connect to Prior ➤
Knowledge of
Math

Use before **LEARN** 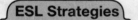 10 MIN

Distribute grid paper to students. Have students color in 1 square. **Each side of this square has a length of 1 unit. What is the perimeter of this square?** *(4 units)* **When we talk about the perimeter, we use units. When we talk about area, we use square units. The area of this square is 1 square unit.** Write the word "area" and the phrase "square unit" on the board, and have students repeat them with you.

Have students draw a square with each side 2 units long. Then have them lightly shade the interior of the square. **You have just colored in a polygon. How many square units did you color?** *(4)* **So the area of this polygon is 4 square units.** Have students draw a square with each side 3 units long and then lightly color in the square. **What is the area of that polygon?** *(9 square units)* Have students draw a rectangle with a length of 4 units and a width of 2 units. Have them color in the rectangle. **What is the area of the polygon?** *(8 square units)*

Problem-Solving Strategy: Act It Out

ACCESS CONTENT

Objective Some problems can be solved by showing the action with objects.

Materials *(per student)* Tiles (Teaching Tool 14)

ESL Strategies *Use before* **CHECK ✓**　　　　🕙 10–15 MIN

Use ➤
Demonstration

Write the following problem on the board and then read it aloud.

> Pablo has some floor tiles. Each tile is 1 foot on each side. Pablo wants to use some tiles to cover his kitchen floor. The area of the floor is 48 square feet. The perimeter of the floor is 28 feet. What is the length and width of Pablo's kitchen floor?

Display 48 square tiles on a desktop in piles. **We can use square tiles to model the problem. What do we know from the problem**? *(The area of the floor is 48 ft² and the perimeter is 28 feet)*. **What do we want to find out?** *(The length and width of the floor)* **How can we arrange the tiles to show this?** Invite volunteers to arrange the tiles into rows until the two criteria of area and perimeter have been met. Provide some guidance by telling students that in this case, the shape of the floor is not a square. It is a rectangle. Therefore two of the sides will measure the same length and two of the other sides will measure the same width. **What is the length and width?** *(8 feet × 6 feet)*

Use Manipulatives ➤
Replace 48 and 28 in the problem on the board with 24 and 20. Have students use their tiles to find the new length and width. *(6 feet × 4 feet)*

Volume

ACCESS CONTENT

Objective Find the volume of rectangular prisms and irregular rectangular solids by counting cubic units or by using a formula.

Materials Ones models from Place-Value Blocks (Teaching Tool 2)

Vocabulary Volume

ESL Strategies *Use before* **LEARN**　　　　🕙 10–15 MIN

Use ➤
Demonstration

On a desktop, use ones models to make a rectangular prism that is 4 cubes long, 2 cubes wide, and 3 cubes high. **We can count cubes to find the <u>volume</u> of this rectangular prism. When we talk about volume, we use cubic units.** Count the cubes one by one. **There is a faster way to find the volume. We can use multiplication.** Write the following sentences on the board.

The length is ____ units. The width is ____ units. The height is ____ units.

The volume is ____ × ____ × ____ cube units.

The volume is ____ cubic units.

Point to the length of the rectangular prism. **This is the length.** Repeat for the width and the height. Then invite volunteers to come to the front of the room, one at a time, and count the number of units in each of the dimensions. Ask them to fill in the values in the sentences on the board. Then ask volunteers to multiply using the Associative Property. **Which two factors did you multiply first?** *(Answers will vary.)* **How did you multiply to find the volume?** *(I multiplied the product of the first two factors by the third factor.)*

Problem-Solving Applications:
Tall Buildings

USE WITH LESSON
8-14

ACCESS CONTENT

Objective Review and apply key concepts, skills, and strategies learned in this and previous chapters.

ESL Strategies > *Use before* **LEARN**   ⏱ 5 MIN

Use Pictures ➤ Read aloud the following word problem, excluding the answer, and then write it on the board.

> The base of John's house is a square. Each side of his house is 40 feet long. The base of Sue's house is also a square. Each side of her house is 45 feet long. What is the difference between the perimeter of John's house and the perimeter of Sue's house?

Have students work together to solve the problem, first drawing pictures to show the perimeters of both houses and then calculating the difference. Ask volunteers to show their pictures to the class and explain how they solved the problem.

Parts of a Region

ACCESS CONTENT

USE WITH LESSON 9-1

Objective Identify and draw fractional parts of a region.

Materials *(per student)* 1 paper circle; 2 paper rectangles

Vocabulary Fraction, numerator, denominator

ESL Strategies **Use before** **LEARN** 🕐 15 MIN

Use Demonstration ➤ Trace a circle on the board. **How many parts are in this circle?** *(1)* **That's right, it has 1 part. It is a whole circle.** Trace another circle and divide it into 2 equal parts. **How many parts does this circle have?** *(2)* **Are the 2 parts the same size and shape?** *(Yes)* **When 2 parts are the same we say that they are equal parts. Each of these equal parts is called 1 half of the whole circle. This circle is divided into 2 halves. A part of the whole circle is also called a** <u>fraction</u> **of the circle. We can use numerals to show the fraction 1 half. The two parts are equal, so we call each part half. This circle is divided into 2 halves.** Write $\frac{1}{2}$ on the board. $\frac{1}{2}$ **is a fraction.**

Trace a third circle and divide it into 2 unequal parts. **How many parts does this circle have?** *(2)* **Are the parts equal?** *(No)* **The parts are not equal, so is the circle is not divided into halves?** *(No)*

Use Manipulatives ➤ Give each student one circle and two rectangles. Have each student fold his or her circle into 2 equal parts. **Fold your circle again to make 4 equal parts.** If necessary, model how to do this for students. After students have done this, say: **Now there are 4 equal parts. Each part is called a fourth. What fraction can we write to show 1 fourth?** $(\frac{1}{4})$ Write $\frac{1}{4}$ on the board. Have students mark each section of their circles $\frac{1}{4}$.

Help students fold one rectangle into thirds and sixths. Then help them fold the second rectangle into ninths. Write the three fractions, $\frac{1}{3}, \frac{1}{6},$ and $\frac{1}{9}$ on the board. Then have students label each third with the fraction $\frac{1}{3}$ on one side of the first rectangle, and each sixth with the fraction $\frac{1}{6}$ on the other side. Then have them label each ninth of the second rectangle with the fraction $\frac{1}{9}$. Point to the <u>numerator</u> of one fraction. **In a fraction, the top number is called the numerator.** Point to the <u>denominator</u>. **The bottom number is called the denominator.**

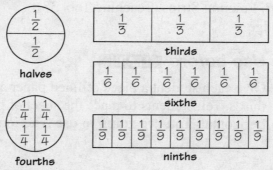

Parts of a Set

ACCESS CONTENT

Objective Identify fractional parts of sets or groups and divide sets to show fractional parts.

Materials 12 pieces of red, yellow, and white chalk; *(per group)* index cards; variety of small classroom materials such as pens, geometric figures, pencils

Vocabulary Fraction, numerator, denominator

ESL Strategies *Use before* **LEARN**   ⏱ 10–15 MIN

Use Real Objects ➤ Display 12 pieces of red, yellow, and white chalk grouped together, preferably in a box. (Do not show the same number of each color.) Explain that the pieces of chalk, grouped together, can be called a set. **How many pieces of chalk are in this set?** *(12 pieces)* Record the number on the board. **How many pieces of each color are in this set?** Record the three counts on the board. **You learned that a <u>fraction</u> can name part of a whole. A fraction can also name a part of a set.** Lead a discussion to determine what fractions name the red, yellow, and white parts of the set of chalk. **What part of a fraction tells how many pieces of chalk are in the whole set?** *(The <u>denominator</u>)* **What part of a fraction tells how many pieces of chalk are in one part of the set?** *(The <u>numerator</u>)*

Use Small-Group Interactions ➤ Assign students to groups. Distribute an index card and a variety of classroom objects to each group. (See the Materials list.) Model with one group how to arrange items into a set. For example, put pencils and chalk together and call them a set. **What fraction of this set is chalk?** Ask each group to form its own set of items and to decide what fractions name the parts of the set. Have one person in each group write the fractions on an index card. Invite each group to show its set to the class. Have a volunteer from each group write on the board the fractions represented by the sets.

Fractions, Length, and the Number Line

ACCESS CONTENT/EXTEND LANGUAGE

Objective Locate and name fractions on a number line.

Materials *(per student)* Fraction Strips (Teaching Tool 38); lined paper; straight edge

ESL Strategies *Use before* **LEARN**   ⏱ 5–10 MIN

Use Manipulatives ➤ Give each student a piece of lined paper and fraction strips for halves and thirds. Tell students to place the sheet of paper so that the lines are horizontal. **You are going to use fraction strips to draw number lines.**

Demonstrate how to place the fraction strip for halves on a line of the paper. Have students mark and label tick marks for 0, $\frac{1}{2}$, and 1 on the number line. When they are done, have them point to each mark on their number lines and read its label aloud. **What do you notice?** *(The number line is divided into two equal parts. The number line shows halves.)*

Repeat the activity using the fraction strip for thirds.

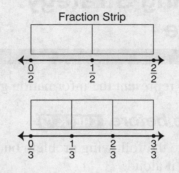

Fraction Strip

Have Students Report Back in Writing ➤ Have students describe in their math journals the way in which they completed the fraction strip activity. On the board, write key vocabulary words, such as "fraction," "half," "halves," "third," and "thirds" for students to refer to. Prompt students with such questions as: **Tell what a number line is. What did you show on your number lines?**

Estimating Fractional Parts

USE WITH LESSON 9-4

ACCESS CONTENT

Objective Estimate fractional parts of regions and sets and estimate fractions for points on a number line.

Materials Clear plastic cup; sand (you may substitute water, rice, or other available material that pours easily)

Vocabulary Benchmark fractions

ESL Strategies ⎞ ***Use before*** **LEARN**　　　　　　　　　　🕐 5 MIN

Use Demonstration ➤ Show the empty cup to the class. **This cup is now empty.** Invite a volunteer to fill about one-fourth of the cup with sand. **About one-fourth of the cup is full.** Stress the word *about* here and in following statements. Write $\frac{1}{4}$ on the board.

Have another volunteer add more sand to the cup so that it is about half full. **About how much of the cup is full now?** *(About half)* Write $\frac{1}{2}$ on the board.

Have a third volunteer add more sand to the cup so that it is about three-fourths full. **About how much of the cup is full now?** *(About three-fourths)* Write $\frac{3}{4}$ on the board. **These fractions are called <u>benchmark fractions</u>. What do we do when we make an estimate of something?** *(We make a reasonable guess about it.)* **Benchmark fractions are those fractions most commonly used when making estimates.** Write the term "benchmark fractions" on the board and have students repeat it with you. Then say with the students: $\frac{1}{4}$, $\frac{1}{2}$, and $\frac{3}{4}$ **are benchmark fractions.**

Have students work with a partner to make simple drawings of three empty cups. Then have the pairs simulate the previous demonstration by taking turns shading in one-fourth, one-half, and three-fourths of the cups. Each time, have them ask each other, "About how much of the cup is full now?"

Problem-Solving Strategy: Draw a Picture

USE WITH LESSON
9-5

EXTEND LANGUAGE

Objective Draw pictures to represent the information given in problems.

ESL Strategies | *Use before* **CHECK** ✓

⏱ 10 MIN

Have Students ➤
Report Back
Orally

Write the following problem on the board, excluding the answer, and then read it aloud.

> Eng built a fence that is 8 feet long. There is a post at each end and at every foot in between. How many posts did Eng use? *(9)*

Write each of the following questions on the board, excluding answers. Ask the following questions: **What information do you know is given in the problem?** *(The fence is 8 feet long. Posts were placed at each end and at each foot.)* **What information are you trying to find?** *(The number of posts used)*

Have students draw a picture to help them solve the problem. Then invite them to talk about how they made their drawing and used it to solve the problem. (If students have trouble with complete sentences, encourage them to use such short phrases as *posts at ends*.) You might also ask volunteers to draw their pictures on the board.

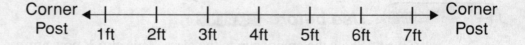

Corner
Post ← | 1ft | 2ft | 3ft | 4ft | 5ft | 6ft | 7ft → Corner
Post

Equivalent Fractions

ACCESS CONTENT

Objective Identify fractions that are equivalent and find fractions equivalent to a given fraction using models and/or a computational procedure.

Materials Quart container; water; 2 pint containers; 4 cup containers

Vocabulary Equivalent fractions

ESL Strategies | *Use before* **LEARN** | ⏱ 5–10 MIN

Use Real Objects ➤ Fill the quart container with water. Have two volunteers come to the front of the room. **You two want to share this water equally.** Pour the water in equal amounts into the 2 pint containers and ask: **Is the water divided evenly?** *(Yes)* **How many containers are there?** *(2)* Write 2 on the board. **How many containers does each person have?** *(1)* On the board, add 1 and a fraction bar to make $\frac{1}{2}$. **What fraction of the water does each person have?** *($\frac{1}{2}$)*

Have each student pour his or her water evenly into 2 of the 4 cup containers. **How many containers are there?** *(4)* Write 4 on the board. **How many containers does each person have?** *(2)* On the board, add a 2 and a fraction bar to make $\frac{2}{4}$. **What fraction of the water does each person have now?** *($\frac{2}{4}$)* **Is this the same amount of water he or she had before?** *(Yes)* **What can you say about $\frac{1}{2}$ and $\frac{2}{4}$?** *(They are equal.)* **When two fractions are the same, or equal, they are called** equivalent fractions. Write the term "equivalent fractions" on the board, and say it aloud with students. Then say with students: $\frac{1}{2}$ **and** $\frac{2}{4}$ **are equivalent fractions.**

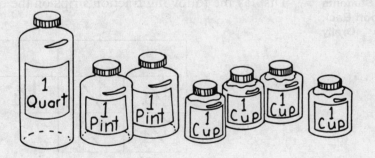

Fractions in Simplest Form

EXTEND LANGUAGE; ACCESS CONTENT

Objective Express fractions in simplest form.

Materials *(per student)* 2 blank index cards; 1 index card labeled "yes," 1 index card labeled "no"

Vocabulary Common factor, simplest form

Use before **CHECK** ✓

⏱ 5 MIN

Focus on Meaning ➤ **How can you tell when a fraction is in <u>simplest form</u>?** *(When the only <u>common factor</u> of the numerator and the denominator is 1)* **If a fraction is in simplest form, you cannot divide the numerator and denominator by any other number than 1.** Write $\frac{4}{8}$ on the board. **Is $\frac{4}{8}$ in simplest form?** *(No)* **How do you know?** *(4 and 8 can both be divided by 2.)* Write $\frac{2}{3}$. **Is $\frac{2}{3}$ in simplest form?** *(Yes)* **How do you know?** *(Because the only number that both 2 and 3 can be divided by is 1)* Repeat with other fractions, such as $\frac{2}{3}$, $\frac{10}{15}$, $\frac{1}{4}$, $\frac{2}{6}$, $\frac{6}{7}$, $\frac{3}{9}$, and $\frac{5}{10}$. Have students give the simplest form of each fraction.

Use Small-Group ➤ Assign students to groups. Each student in the group should write one
Interactions fraction that is in simplest form and one fraction that is not on each of his or her blank index cards. Students should take turns holding up a card while the other students decide whether it is in simplest form or not. If it is, students hold up a "yes" card. If it is not, they hold up a "no" card. For each "no," one student must tell why the fraction is not in simplest form.

Using Number Sense to Compare Fractions

USE WITH LESSON
9-8

EXTEND LANGUAGE

Objective Determine which of two fractions is greater (or less).

Materials Overhead fraction strips

Use before **CHECK** ✓

⏱ 10 MIN

Have Students ➤ Display the following fraction strips on the overhead.
Report Back
Orally

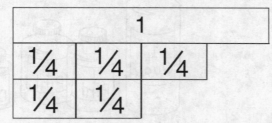

Ask students to work with a partner to decide which of the two fractions is greater. Call on students to report back by naming the greater fraction ($\frac{3}{4}$) and then explaining how they made that determination. Repeat with other fraction combinations.

Comparing and Ordering Fractions

USE WITH LESSON 9-9

ACTIVATE PRIOR KNOWLEDGE/BUILD BACKGROUND; ACCESS CONTENT

Objective Compare fractions using >, <, and =, and order fractions.

Materials Overhead fraction strips; *(per student)* Fraction Strips (Teaching Tool 38); index card marked with a fraction with a denominator of 10 or less

ESL Strategies   ***Use before*** **LEARN**   ⏱ 10–15 MIN

Connect to Prior Experiences ➤ Display overhead fraction strips for $\frac{2}{3}$ and $\frac{1}{4}$, aligning them at the left. Tell students to imagine that the fraction strips are granola bars or something else they like to eat. **Which would you rather have, two thirds of a bar or one fourth of a bar?** *($\frac{2}{3}$ bar)* **Why?** *(Because it's bigger)* **That's right: $\frac{2}{3}$ is greater than $\frac{1}{4}$.** Write $\frac{2}{3} > \frac{1}{4}$ on the board. **Which bar is the smaller piece?** *($\frac{1}{4}$ bar)* **That means that $\frac{1}{4}$ is less than $\frac{2}{3}$.** Write $\frac{1}{4} < \frac{2}{3}$ on the board. Have students read each inequality aloud. Repeat the activity with other fraction pairs until students are comfortable identifying the greater and lesser fraction in each pair.

Use Small-Group Interactions ➤ Group students in pairs. Have each pair choose two fraction cards and compare the two fractions using fraction strips. Then have students write two number sentences to show the comparisons, one using the less-than symbol and one using the greater-than symbol. Students then read the sentences aloud.

Mixed Numbers and Improper Fractions

USE WITH LESSON 9-10

ACTIVATE PRIOR KNOWLEDGE/BUILD BACKGROUND; ACCESS CONTENT

Objective Read, write, and show mixed numbers, express mixed numbers as improper fractions, and improper fractions as mixed numbers.

Materials *(per group)* Paper circle pattern; scissors

Vocabulary Mixed numbers

ESL Strategies   ***Use before*** **LEARN**   ⏱ 10–15 MIN

Connect to Prior Knowledge of Math ➤ Write $\frac{1}{2}$ on the board. **Is this is a fraction or a whole number?** *(Fraction)* Write 1 on the board. **Is this is a fraction or a whole number?** *(Whole number)* Write $1\frac{1}{2}$ on the board. **This is a <u>mixed number</u>.** Ask students to tell why they think $1\frac{1}{2}$ is called a mixed number. *(Sample answer: It has both a whole number and a fraction.)*

On the board, draw circles as shown in the following illustration and say: **You can use circles to show $\frac{1}{2}$, 1, and $1\frac{1}{2}$.**

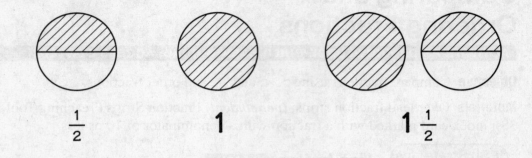

$$\frac{1}{2} \qquad\qquad 1 \qquad\qquad 1\frac{1}{2}$$

Use Small-Group Interactions ➤ Assign students to groups. Give each group a paper circle pattern and a pair of scissors. Have each group trace and cut out 6 circles. With one group, model folding and cutting circles to show $\frac{1}{2}$ and $1\frac{1}{2}$. Challenge groups to show $1\frac{1}{8}$, $1\frac{1}{4}$, $1\frac{3}{4}$, and $2\frac{1}{2}$ using the circles. As each circle model is displayed, ask students to name the mixed number it shows.

Comparing Mixed Numbers

USE WITH LESSON 9-11

ACCESS CONTENT

Objective Compare mixed numbers.

ESL Strategies *Use before* CHECK ✓   ⏱ 10 MIN

Use Graphic Organizers ➤ Write the following headings on the board. Ask students to copy them in their notebooks.

Less Than (<)   Mixed Number   Greater Than (>)

Under "Mixed Number," write $2\frac{1}{2}$. Ask a volunteer to tell you if $1\frac{1}{2}$ is less than $2\frac{1}{2}$ or greater than $2\frac{1}{2}$. *(Less than $2\frac{1}{2}$)* Write $1\frac{1}{2}$ in the first column, and have students do the same. Then ask another volunteer to tell you if $3\frac{1}{8}$ is less than $2\frac{1}{2}$ or greater than $2\frac{1}{2}$. *(Greater than $2\frac{1}{2}$)* Write $3\frac{1}{8}$ in the third column, and have the students do the same.

Write the following mixed numbers in the center column under $2\frac{1}{2}$: $3\frac{1}{4}$, $1\frac{9}{10}$, $6\frac{1}{3}$, $4\frac{5}{6}$. Have students work in pairs to identify mixed numbers that are less than and greater than each, and to write them in the proper columns. Invite pairs to share the mixed numbers they noted with the class. Correct or confirm each example the students cite.

Circle Graphs

Objective Read a circle graph to find information needed to solve problems.

Materials Colored chalk; *(per group)* paper circle pattern; crayons

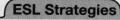 **ESL Strategies**

Use before **LEARN**

🕐 10–15 MIN

Use
Demonstration
➤ Draw a circle on the board. Shade $\frac{1}{2}$ of it red, $\frac{1}{4}$ yellow, $\frac{1}{8}$ blue, and $\frac{1}{8}$ green. **How much of the circle is red?** $(\frac{1}{2})$ **How much is yellow?** $(\frac{1}{4})$ **Blue?** $(\frac{1}{8})$ **Green?** $(\frac{1}{8})$

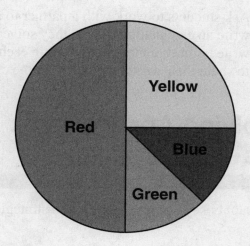

Use
Peer Questioning
➤ Assign students to groups, and give each group paper, a circle pattern, and some crayons. Have students trace and cut out 3 circles. Model with one group folding a circle in half and then folding the halved circle in thirds to form sixths. **Color $\frac{1}{2}$ of your circle green.** Give students time to color each portion before you give the next direction. **Now color $\frac{1}{3}$ of your circle blue. Finally, color $\frac{1}{6}$ of your circle brown.**

Have groups fold a second circle into 6 equal sections. Then have them color the sections any way they like. Use the example to remind them that two or more sections next to each other may be the same color.

Have students take turns hiding their circles while another group asks questions such as, "What fraction of the circle is the largest part?" and "What color is it?" As questioning continues, the group asking questions reproduces the other group's circle. When circles are complete, groups reveal their original circles, and the two are compared.

Problem-Solving Skill: Writing to Explain

EXTEND LANGUAGE

USE WITH LESSON 9-13

Objective Write to explain an estimate.

ESL Strategies

Use before **LEARN**

⏱ 10 MIN

> Have Students Report Back in Writing

Write the following word problem, excluding the answer, on the board. Read the problem to students.

> Carlos has 103 stamps. About $\frac{1}{2}$ of them are U.S. stamps. About how many of Carlos's stamps are not U.S. stamps? *(About 50 stamps)*

Ask students to work with a partner to solve the problem. Invite each pair to write an explanation of how they solved the problem. Encourage students to write number sentences to explain each step in their answer. Invite volunteers to share their written reports with the class.

Problem-Solving Applications: Coral Reefs

ACCESS CONTENT

USE WITH LESSON 9-14

Objective Review and apply key concepts, skills, and strategies learned in this and previous chapters.

ESL Strategies

Use before **LEARN**

⏱ 5 MIN

> Use Small-Group Interactions

Read aloud the following word problem, excluding the answer, and then write it on the board.

> Maria and her family are going on vacation to the coral reefs. She made a circle graph showing the vacation budget. The family will spend $\frac{1}{2}$ of the vacation money for airfare, $\frac{1}{4}$ of the money for food and hotel, and $\frac{1}{4}$ of the money for sightseeing. **What does Maria's circle graph look like?** *($\frac{1}{2}$ of the circle is labeled Airfare, $\frac{1}{4}$ of the circle is labeled Food and Hotel, and $\frac{1}{4}$ of the circle is labeled Sightseeing)*

Have students work together to draw the circle graph. They should first divide a circle in half, and then divide one of the halves in half again. Finally, students should label each section of the graph with the appropriate budget fraction and category.

Estimating Fraction Sums

USE WITH LESSON 10-1

ACCESS CONTENT

Objective Estimate sums of fractions.

Materials *(per pair)* Fraction Strips (Teaching Tool 38)

ESL Strategies

Use before **LEARN**

⏱ 5–10 MIN

Use Demonstration ➤ Write $\frac{1}{3} + \frac{3}{6}$ ___ 1 on the board. Then show fraction strips for $\frac{1}{3}$, $\frac{3}{6}$, and 1. **Is the sum equal to 1?** *(No)* **Is the sum greater than 1?** *(No)* **Is the sum less than 1?** *(Yes)* Erase the blank and write < in its place. **Read the complete number sentence out loud.** *($\frac{1}{3} + \frac{3}{6}$ is less than 1.)*

Use Small-Group Interactions ➤ Write the following, excluding answers, on the board.

$$\frac{1}{2} + \frac{1}{4} \underline{\quad} 1 \ (<) \qquad \frac{5}{8} + \frac{3}{4} \underline{\quad} 1 \ (>) \qquad \frac{4}{6} + \frac{1}{3} \underline{\quad} 1 \ (=)$$

Distribute fraction strips to pairs of students, and have them use the strips to determine if each sum is equal to 1, greater than 1, or less than 1. Then ask each pair to record their results and report their findings to the class.

Adding Fractions with Like Denominators

USE WITH LESSON 10-2

ACTIVATE PRIOR KNOWLEDGE\BUILD BACKGROUND; ACCESS CONTENT

Objective Add fractions with like denominators, using models and paper and pencil.

ESL Strategies

Use before **LEARN**

⏱ 10–15 MIN

Connect to Prior Knowledge of Math ➤ On the board, draw three circles: one divided into halves, one divided into thirds, and one divided into fourths. Ask volunteers to shade $\frac{1}{2}$ of the first circle, $\frac{2}{3}$ of the second circle, and $\frac{2}{4}$ of the third circle. **What fraction names the part of the first circle that is *not* shaded?** *($\frac{1}{2}$)* **How do you know?** *(There are 2 equal parts, and 1 part is shaded; 2 − 1 = 1 part not shaded, or $\frac{1}{2}$)* **What fraction names the part of the second circle that is *not* shaded?** *($\frac{1}{3}$)* **How do you know?** *(There are 3 equal parts, and 2 parts are shaded; 3 − 2 = 1 part not shaded, or $\frac{1}{3}$)* **What fraction names the part of the third circle that is not shaded?** *($\frac{2}{4}$ or $\frac{1}{2}$)* **How do you know?** *(There are 4 equal parts, and 2 parts are shaded; 4 − 2 = 2 parts not shaded, or $\frac{2}{4}$; $\frac{2}{4} = \frac{1}{2}$)*

Use Pictures ➤ Write the following problems on the board. Invite students to read aloud each problem with you.

1. Sam ordered a pizza with green peppers on $\frac{1}{4}$ of it and olives on a different $\frac{1}{4}$. How much of the pizza had toppings?

2. Margo ordered a pizza with sausage on $\frac{1}{3}$ of it and peppers on a different $\frac{1}{3}$. How much of the pizza had toppings?

3. Mario ordered a pizza with mushrooms on $\frac{1}{4}$ and broccoli on a different $\frac{2}{4}$. How much of the pizza had toppings?

Draw another circle on the board, divide it into fourths, and have students copy it. Reread the first problem aloud. **What do we know?** *(The pizza was topped with $\frac{1}{4}$ green peppers and $\frac{1}{4}$ olives.)* Tell students to shade $\frac{1}{4}$ of the circle as you do the same on the board. **$\frac{1}{4}$ of the pizza had green peppers.** Then have them shade another $\frac{1}{4}$ as you do. **A different $\frac{1}{4}$ had olives. What operation do we use to find how much of the pizza had toppings altogether?** *(Addition)* **How much of your pizza is shaded?** *($\frac{2}{4}$, or $\frac{1}{2}$)* **That's right. $\frac{1}{4} + \frac{1}{4} = \frac{2}{4}$. So $\frac{2}{4}$, or $\frac{1}{2}$, of the pizza had toppings.** Then have students draw pictures to solve the remaining two problems.

Jenny, color the circle to show $\frac{1}{2}$

Adding Fractions with Unlike Denominators

ACCESS CONTENT

USE WITH LESSON 10-3

Objective Add fractions with unlike denominators using models and paper and pencil.

ESL Strategies **Use before** **LEARN**   🕐 10 MIN

Use ➤ Demonstration Write the following problem on the board. Invite students to read the problem with you.

Mr. Ling wants to make some wooden toys. He has two pieces of wood to use. One piece of wood is $\frac{1}{8}$ yard long, and the other piece is $\frac{1}{2}$ yard long. How much wood does Mr. Ling have?

What do we need to do to solve the problem? *(Add $\frac{1}{8}$ yd + $\frac{1}{2}$ yd.)* Write $\frac{1}{8} + \frac{1}{2} = $ ____ on the board. **What part of a fraction is the denominator?** *(The bottom part)* **Which number in the first fraction is the denominator?** *(8)* **Which number in the second fraction is the denominator?** *(2)* **Are the two denominators the same?** *(No)* **How can we add fractions with different denominators?** *(Find equivalent fractions.)* **We can use number lines to find equivalent fractions.** Display the three number lines shown below.

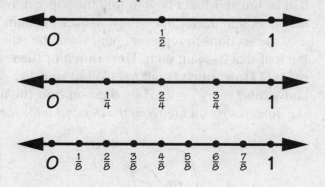

Write $\frac{1}{2}$ on the board. **What fraction is equal to $\frac{1}{2}$ and has a denominator of 8?** *($\frac{4}{8}$)* Write $\frac{1}{2} = \frac{4}{8}$ on the board. **What addition sentence can we write now?** *($\frac{1}{8} + \frac{4}{8} = $ __)* Ask a volunteer to locate $\frac{1}{8}$ on one of the number lines. Then ask him or her to count on $\frac{4}{8}$. **What is $\frac{1}{8} + \frac{4}{8}$?** *($\frac{5}{8}$)* **So Mr. Ling has $\frac{5}{8}$ yd of wood.**

Subtracting Fractions with Like Denominators

USE WITH LESSON
10-4

ACTIVATE PRIOR KNOWLEDGE\BUILD BACKGROUND

Objective Subtract fractions with like denominators using models and paper and pencil.

Materials *(per pair)* 2 sheets of paper; pencil; scissors

ESL Strategies | *Use before* **LEARN**   🕐 5–10 MIN

Use Simulation ➤ Group students in pairs and give each pair 2 sheets of paper, a pencil, and scissors. Hold up a sheet of paper and tell students that it represents a loaf of bread. **You are going to divide this bread into 6 slices. What part of the bread is each slice?** *($\frac{1}{6}$)*

Model how to divide the paper into 6 sections by folding it in half one way and then in thirds the other way. Have the first student in each pair fold 1 sheet of paper and then write $\frac{1}{6}$ in each section. **Now we're going to put peanut butter on 2 of these slices.** Have the student shade 2 sections to represent the peanut butter. **How much of the loaf has peanut butter on it?** *($\frac{2}{6}$)*

Tell the second student in each pair to cut off the part with the peanut butter on it. **How much of the bread is left?** *($\frac{4}{6}$)* On the board, write $\frac{6}{6} - \frac{2}{6} = \frac{4}{6}$. Read the equation aloud, and point to the appropriate numbers as you say: **When the denominators are the same, find the difference by subtracting the numerators.**

Hold up a second piece of paper and tell students that it represents another loaf of bread. Model how to fold the paper into thirds. Have one partner fold the sheet into thirds and write $\frac{1}{3}$ in each section. Then have him or her shade 2 of the sections to represent jam. Have the other partner cut off the part of the loaf that has jam on it. **How much of the second loaf of bread was cut off?** *($\frac{2}{3}$)* **How much is left?** *($\frac{1}{3}$)* **What number sentence can we write to show this?** *($\frac{3}{3} - \frac{2}{3} = \frac{1}{3}$)* **How did you find the difference?** *(By subtracting the numerators and leaving the denominator the same)*

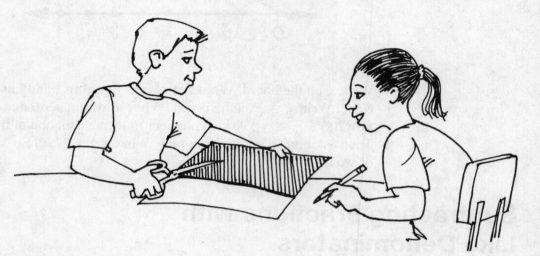

Subtracting Fractions with Unlike Denominators

ACTIVATE PRIOR KNOWLEDGE\BUILD BACKGROUND

USE WITH LESSON
10-5

Objective Subtract fractions with unlike denominators using models and paper and pencil.

ESL Strategies **Use before** **LEARN**

🕐 5 MIN

Connect to Prior ➢
Knowledge of
Math

Write the following problem on the board and then read it aloud.

A builder has a piece of wood that is $\frac{1}{3}$ foot long. He cuts and removes a piece that is $\frac{1}{6}$ foot long. How much wood is left?

What do we need to do to solve the problem? *(Subtract $\frac{1}{6}$ from $\frac{1}{3}$.)* **What number sentence can we write to show that?** *($\frac{1}{3} - \frac{1}{6} = $ ____)* **Which number in the first fraction is the denominator?** *(3)* **In the second fraction?** *(6)* **Are the denominators the same?** *(No)*

Display number lines that show equivalents among thirds and sixths. Remind students of the work they did with number lines to solve fraction addition problems. Ask a volunteer to come forward and use the number lines to rename $\frac{1}{3}$ as a fraction with a denominator of 6. ($\frac{2}{6}$) Have another student perform the subtraction and write the answer on the board. ($\frac{1}{6}$)

Problem-Solving Strategy: Use Logical Reasoning

USE WITH LESSON 10-6

ACCESS CONTENT

Objective Use the information given in the problem to make conclusions.

ESL Strategies *Use before* **CHECK ✓**   ⏱ 5–10 MIN

Use Graphic Organizers ➤ Write the following problem on the board, and then read it aloud.

> The ages of three children are 3, 4, and 5. Sue is not 4 years old. Carlos is 3 years old. How old is Jan?

Draw the following table on the board.

	3	4	5
Sue			
Carlos			
Jan			

What do you know? *(Sue is not 4 years old. Carlos is 3 years old.)* **What are you trying to find?** *(Jan's age)*

Ask a volunteer to help you model using the table to solve the problem. Have the volunteer follow each instruction. **Sue is not 4 years old. Let's write "no" in that box. Carlos *is* 3 years old. Let's write "yes" in that box. What ages are not Carlos's age?** *(4 and 5)* **What should we write in each of those boxes?** *(No)* **Can Sue be 3?** *(No)* **What should we write in that box?** *(No)* **How old is Sue?** *(5)* **What should we write in that box?** *(Yes)* **If Carlos is 3 and Sue is 5, how is Jan?** *(4)* **What should we write in the boxes for Jan?** *(No; Yes; No)*

Length and Customary Units

ACCESS CONTENT

Objective Estimate and measure length to the nearest inch, and choose the most appropriate customary unit of length for a given object or distance.

Vocabulary Inch, foot, yard, mile

ESL Strategies *Use before* **CHECK ✓** 🕑 5–10 MIN

Use Graphic Organizers ➤ Draw four word webs on the board. Start with four center ovals, one labeled "About an <u>Inch</u>," another labeled "About a <u>Foot</u>," another labeled "About a <u>Yard</u>," and the last labeled "About a <u>Mile</u>."

Help students brainstorm things whose lengths, widths, or heights are about equal to each of the customary units of measure. As words are called out, write them into ovals surrounding the appropriate web. Give students feedback. When a suggestion is inappropriate to a given unit, use a yardstick to help students visualize the length of the object (except in the case of mile). As an alternative to having students call out words, you might have volunteers come to the board one at a time and write their suggestions directly in the web. You may also have students draw pictures in the web that stand for the words.

Fractions of an Inch

ACCESS CONTENT

Objective Measure and draw lengths to the nearest half, quarter, or eighth of an inch.

Materials Overhead ruler; piece of chalk about $1\frac{1}{2}$ in. long; *(per student)* inch ruler

ESL Strategies *Use before* **LEARN** 🕑 10 MIN

Use Demonstration ➤ Display the Overhead ruler. Point to the distance between 0 and 1. **What measurement does this show?** *(1 in.)* Point to the distance between 0 and $\frac{1}{2}$. **What measurement does this show?** *($\frac{1}{2}$ in.)* Hold the piece of chalk above the ruler, with the left edge above the 0-in. mark and the right edge near the $1\frac{1}{2}$-in. mark. **About how long is this piece of chalk?** *(About $1\frac{1}{2}$ in. long)*

Use Manipulatives ➤ Have pairs of students use their inch rulers to find and measure the lengths (or widths or heights) of three or four classroom objects to the nearest inch or $\frac{1}{2}$ inch. Then ask each pair to record their results and then to report them to another pair of students.

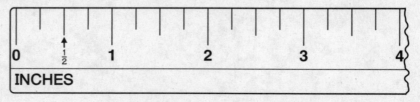

98 Chapter 10

Capacity and Customary Units

EXTEND LANGUAGE

Objective Choose the most appropriate customary unit of capacity for a given container, and estimate and measure capacity using customary units.

Materials Containers: cup, pint, quart, gallon

Vocabulary Capacity, cup, pint, quart, gallon

ESL Strategies *Use before* **LEARN**   🕐 10–15 MIN

Focus on Meaning ➤ On the board write the words "cup," "pint," "quart," and "gallon." **These words name different sized containers. We use containers to hold or measure things.** Hold up a cup container, point to the word "cup" on the board, and say: **This is a cup.** Have students say the word with you. Repeat with the remaining containers. **What kinds of things do you measure in cups, pints, quarts, or gallons?** *(Answers may vary; liquids)*

Write the word "capacity" on the board. Explain that capacity is the amount a container can hold. Hold up the cup container. **The capacity of this container is 1 c.** Draw a cup container on the board as shown in the illustration below. Then hold up the pint container and say: **What is the capacity of this container?** *(1 pt)* **A pint is the same as 2 c.** Draw 2 c on the board as shown below. Continue for quarts and gallons.

Ask such questions as: **How many cups are in 1 qt?** *(4)* Offer situational problems, such as: **I need half a gallon of milk. There are no half-gallon containers at the store. What can I buy instead?** *(2 qt; 4 pt; or 1 qt and 2 pt)*

Have students add the terms *cup, pint, quart,* and *gallon* to their math dictionaries.

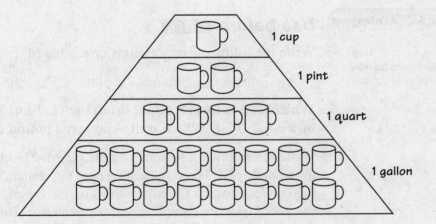

Weight and Customary Units

ACTIVATE PRIOR KNOWLEDGE\BUILD BACKGROUND; EXTEND LANGUAGE

Objective Choose the most appropriate customary unit of weight for a given object, and estimate and measure weight using customary units.

Materials *(per student)* Poster paper; crayons or felt pens

Vocabulary Ounce, pound, ton

ESL Strategies   *Use before* CHECK ✓   5–10 MIN

Connect to Prior Experiences ➤ Write the headings "Ounce," "Pound," and "Ton" on the board.

A box of pencils weighs a few ounces. Write "box of pencils" under "Ounce." **A book weighs a few pounds.** Write "book" under "Pound." **A car weighs a few tons.** Write "car" under "Ton."

Use Demonstration ➤ Have students copy the information from the board onto poster paper. Then ask pairs of students to brainstorm other objects that weigh a few ounces, a few pounds, and a few tons. Have students add these objects to their posters. Invite students to draw pictures if they are not yet familiar with the English words for the objects. Use the posters as part of a bulletin-board display on customary units of measure.

Changing Units and Comparing Measures

ACCESS CONTENT

Objective Change units of length, capacity, and weight to equivalent units and compare measures.

ESL Strategies   *Use before* CHECK ✓   5–10 MIN

Use Demonstration ➤ Write the following expressions on the board.

$$3 \text{ feet} = \underline{\quad} \text{ inches} \quad 2 \text{ pints} = \underline{\quad} \text{ cups} \quad 5 \text{ pounds} = \underline{\quad} \text{ ounces}$$

Which unit is larger, a foot or an inch? *(Foot)* **Which unit is larger, a pint or a cup?** *(Pint)* **Which unit is larger, a pound or an ounce?** *(Pound)*

Write the following sentence on the board: "To change larger units to smaller units, multiply." Have students repeat the sentence after you. Then complete the conversions for the expressions on the board. Have volunteers come to the board to write complete number sentences for each. *(3 ft ×12 = 36 in.; 2 pt × 2 = 4 c; 5 lb × 16 = 80 oz)*

Write the following expressions on the board.

24 inches = ____ feet   8 cups = ____ pints   32 ounces = ____ pounds

Next, write the following sentence on the board and have students repeat it after you: "To change from smaller units to larger units, divide." Then have volunteers come to the board to complete the conversions and write a number sentence for each. *(24 in. ÷ 12 = 2 ft; 8 c ÷ 2 = 4 pt; 32 oz ÷ 16 = 2 lb)*

Problem-Solving Skill: Exact Answer or Estimate

USE WITH LESSON 10-12

EXTEND LANGUAGE; ACCESS CONTENT

Objective Give an exact answer or an estimate depending on what the problem asks.

Materials *(per student)* Index cards labeled "measure" and "estimate"

ESL Strategies *Use before* **LEARN** ⏱ 5–10 MIN

Have Students ➤ Report Back Orally

Distribute two index cards to each student, one labeled "measure" and the other labeled "estimate." **Suppose you bought some things for your home. Listen carefully to each sentence I say that describes the things you buy. Hold up the "measure" card if you need an exact measurement to buy the item. Hold up the "estimate" card if an estimate is OK.** After reading each of the statements aloud, have students discuss why they held up the card they did.

> **You want to buy new carpet for your bedroom.**
>
> **You want to buy a picture frame for a picture.**
>
> **You want to buy some paint to paint your kitchen.**
>
> **You want to buy a fence to put around your yard.**
>
> **You want to buy some seeds for your garden.**

Use ➤ Peer Questioning

Assign students to groups, and have each member write at least two statements like the ones you modeled. In turns, students read their statements. Each time, the other members in the group hold up either the "measure" or "estimate" card and provide rationales for their choices.

Problem-Solving Applications:
The Empire State Building

EXTEND LANGUAGE

Objective Review and apply key concepts, skills, and strategies learned in Chapters 1–10.

Materials *(per group)* Inch ruler

ESL Strategies | *Use before* **LEARN** | ⏱ 10 MIN

Have Students ➤
Report Back
in Writing

Write the following word problem on the board, excluding the answer, and then read it aloud.

Raoul drew a dot on a line. He drew a second dot on the same line $\frac{1}{2}$ inch to the left of the first dot. Then he made another dot on the line $\frac{1}{4}$ inch to the right of the first dot. How far apart are the second and third dots? ($\frac{3}{4}$ *in.*)

Have students work in groups to draw a picture that will help them solve the problem. Have them write down the steps involved in making their drawings and in solving the problem. Tell students they may use numbers as well as steps to describe each step. If possible, assign at least one student to each group who is fluent or very proficient in English. Then have groups share their drawings and their methods for finding the solution with the class.

(Some students may describe solving the problem with computation, while others may describe measuring the distance between the dots after they are drawn.)

Decimals and Fractions

ACCESS CONTENT

USE WITH LESSON
11-1

Objective Relate decimals to common fraction benchmarks, and write decimals in tenths and hundredths.

Materials *(per group)* Bill and Coin Models (Teaching Tool 7)

ESL Strategies

Use Small-Group Interactions ➤

Use before **LEARN**

🕐 5 MIN

Assign students to groups. Give each group two $1-bills and two dollars in coins. Write $1.50 on the board. Have students count out that amount. **How much money is that?** *(1 dollar and 50 cents)* **Can you think of another way to say the same amount?** Allow students to discuss this question in their groups. *(Sample answers: 1 $\frac{1}{2}$ dollars; 1 $\frac{50}{100}$ dollars)* If necessary, provide clues to direct students toward an answer, *(for example:* **How many cents are there in a dollar***)*.

Point to the decimal point in $1.50. **A** *decimal point* **separates the dollars from the cents.** Then point to the 50. **The numbers to the left of the decimal point show the number of dollars. What do the numbers to the right of the decimal point show?** *(The number of cents)* **How many cents are there are 100 cents in a dollar?** *(100)* **So 50 cents is what fraction of a dollar?** *($\frac{50}{100}$)* **That's the same as $\frac{1}{2}$ of a dollar.**

Repeat the activity with $2.25 and $3.75.

Decimal Place Value

ACCESS CONTENT

Objective Write decimals in tenths and hundredths.

Materials Materials *(per group)* 4 sets of cards marked 0–9

ESL Strategies

Use before **LEARN**   ⏱ 10 MIN

Use Total Physical Response ➤ On the board, draw the place-value chart shown in the illustration. Be sure it is large enough for each of four children to stand under, one per separate column. Assign students to groups, and give each group 4 sets of number cards. **You are going to use your number cards to show the numbers I call out. To do that, you will stand under the right place in the chart.** Choose one of the groups. **Two of you come forward to show the mixed decimal 3.6.** The student holding the 3 card must then stand in the ones column, and the student holding the 6 card must stand in the tenths column. Repeat the activity for each of the other groups. Invite a volunteer to write the number indicated in the chart and that you called out. Ask this student to write large numbers that cover an entire sheet of paper and to flash the number to the class.

Then choose mixed decimals in the teens, twenties, and so on, with both tenths and hundredths. Pronounce some numbers one way (for example: fifty-four and thirty-five hundredths) and some numbers the other way (**for example: fifty-four point three five**). Ask more groups of students to demonstrate the number by standing in the appropriate column of the chart.

| Tens | Ones | Tenths | Hundredths |

Comparing and Ordering Decimals

ACTIVATE PRIOR KNOWLEDGE/BUILD BACKGROUND

Objective Write, compare, and order decimals to hundredths.

Materials *(per group)* Bill and Coin Models (Teaching Tool 7)

ESL Strategies

Connect to Prior ➤
Knowledge of
Math

Use before **LEARN**

⏱ 10 MIN

Today we will be using the terms *less than* **and** *greater than*. **We will also be using the symbols that stand for these terms.** Write "greater than (>)" and "less than (<)" on the board.

You have already learned how to use these terms and symbols with whole numbers. What greater than sentence can we write using the numbers 5 and 2? *(5 > 2)* Invite students to write this statement on the board in Column 1 and have the class read it along with you: **5 is greater than 2. What less than sentence can we write using the numbers 5 and 2?** *(2 < 5)* Invite students to write this statement on the board in Column 2 and have the class read it along with you: **2 is less than 5.** Then draw the following items and price tags on the board.

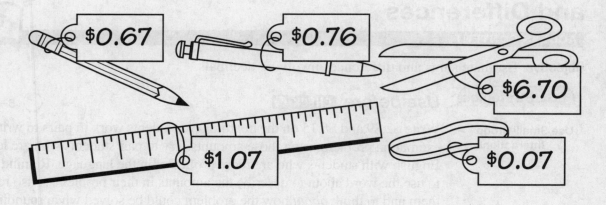

Assign students to groups. Have each group use their play money to show the price of each item. Then have group members ask each other comparison questions such as, "Is $0.67 greater than $1.07 or less than $1.07?" *(Less than)* and "Is $6.70 less than $0.76 or greater than $0.76?" *(Greater than)* Finally, have each group list pairs of comparison statements using the greater than and less than symbols (e.g., $0.67 < $1.07, $6.70 > $0.76). Invite volunteers to write their comparison statements on the board.

Rounding Decimals

EXTEND LANGUAGE

USE WITH LESSON 11-4

Objective Round decimals to the nearest whole number and tenth.

ESL Strategies

Use before **LEARN**　　　　　　　　　🕐 10 MIN

Have Students ➤
Report Back
Orally

Write 2.2, 4.3, and 4.9 on the board. Then draw a number line, and divide it into tenths labeled from 2.0 to 3.0.

Point to the decimal 2.2 on the board and then to the decimallabel 2.2 on at the appropriate place on the number line. **Is 2.2 closer to 2 or closer to 3?** *(2)* Point to 2.0 on the number line and then write 2 on the board.

Change the labels on the number line so that it shows 4.0 to 5.0. Have pairs of students work together to discuss whether 4.3 is closer to 4 or to 5 and then discuss whether 4.9 is closer to 4 or to 5. Have students report back orally by discussing their results with another pair.

Estimating Decimal Sums and Differences

ACCESS CONTENT

USE WITH LESSON 11-5

Objective Estimate sums and differences involving decimals.

ESL Strategies

Use before **CHECK**　　　　　　　　🕐 5–10 MIN

Use Small-Group ➤
Interactions

Write $2.89 and $6.15 on the board. Have students work in pairs to write an estimation problem using those amounts. Try to pair students who are learning English with students who are more proficient in the language. Remind students to use the word about to describe the amounts in their problems. Also remind them and to think *about* how the problem could be solved when rounding the money amounts to the nearest whole dollar.

When everyone has finished writing their problems, have one pair of students exchange problems with another pair to solve. When students have found their solutions, have pairs meet to explain to one another how they solved the problems. Then have the pair who wrote the problem then provides feedback about how they thought the problem would be solved. For example, if students wrote the problem shown, they would confirm that the problem should be solved by adding the price of the book and the price of the CD to find the total amount spent.

I bought a book for $2.98 and a CD for $6.15. About how much did I spend in all?

Using Grids to Add and Subtract Decimals

ACCESS CONTENT; EXTEND LANGUAGE

USE WITH LESSON
11-6

Objective Add and subtract decimals in tenths, hundredths, and combinations of whole numbers, tenths, and hundredths.

Materials *(per pair)* 10 ×10 Grid Paper (Teaching Tool 5); scissors

ESL Strategies

Use before **LEARN**

🕐 10–15 MIN

Use Small-Group Interactions ➤ Give each pair 3 sheets of grid paper and scissors. Write the following problem on the board.

$$
\begin{array}{r}
1.8 \\
-0.6 \\
\hline
\end{array}
$$

Model using grids to show 1.8. Demonstrate the following steps as students follow them. **First shade one whole grid to show 1. Then shade eight columns on another grid to show eight tenths.** Point to the problem on the board. **How much are you going to subtract?** *(0.6 or 6 tenths)* Model cutting 6 columns from the second grid. **I have subtracted 6 tenths from 1 and 8 tenths. What do I have left?** *(1 and 2 tenths)* Write "1 and 2 tenths = 1.2" on the board.

Have Students Report Back Orally ➤ Write the following problem on the board. Have students solve the problem by shading and then cutting their grids. Ask each pair to tell you how they arrived at their answer.

Adding and Subtracting Decimals

ACCESS CONTENT

Objective Add, subtract, and estimate with decimals in tenths, hundredths, and combinations of whole numbers, tenths, and hundredths.

ESL Strategies

Use before CHECK ✓

⏱ 10 MIN

Use ➤ Demonstration

Draw a number line on the board. Divide it into tenths labeled from 0 to 2.0. Beneath it, write the following problem.

$$0.7 + 0.4 = \underline{\hspace{1cm}}$$

We can use a number line to add these two decimals. What is the value of each unit on the number line? *(One tenth)* Ask a volunteer to come to the board and locate 0.7 on the number line. Then have students count on 4 tenths with you as the volunteer moves his or her finger one tenth at a time to the right: **8 tenths, 9 tenths, 10 tenths, 11 tenths.** Then ask students: **Where did we stop?** *(11 tenths)* **What is another name way to say 11 tenths?** *(1.1, or 1 and 1 tenth)*

Rewrite the problem in vertical form. Point to both of the decimal points. **Line up the decimal points. Add the decimals the same way you would add whole numbers.** Continue with other examples. Each time, have one student find the answer using the number line. Have another student write the problem vertically and solve it on the board.

Problem-Solving Strategy: Solve a Simpler Problem

ACCESS CONTENT

Objective Solve hard problems by breaking them apart or changing them into smaller parts.

ESL Strategies

Use before LEARN

⏱ 10 MIN

Use Total ➤ Physical Response

Suppose 8 children meet for the first time. They all shake hands with one another. How many handshakes are there in all? Draw two columns on the board and label them "Number of Children" and "Number of Handshakes." Write 8 near the bottom of the left column and a question mark next to it in the right column.

Write 2 at the top of the left column. **Let's solve a simpler problem first. How many handshakes are there when 2 people meet?** Have two volunteers come to the front of the room and shake hands. Ask for a response from the class and write the answer *(1)* in the right column.

Write 3 below 2 in the left column. **How many handshakes are there when 3 people meet?** Have a third volunteer come to the front of the room, and ask all 3 children to shake hands. Have the class count the handshakes. Then write the answer *(3)* in the right column on the board. Repeat with 4 people *(6 handshakes)* and 5 people *(10 handshakes)*. Be sure that children shake hands one at a time so the children who observe can count each handshake.

Do you see a pattern? *(To find the next number of handshakes, increase the number you add to the number of handshakes to a number that increases by 1: 1 handshake + 2 = 3 handshakes (for 3 people); 3 handshakes + 3 = 6 handshakes (for 4 people); 6 handshakes + 4 = 10 handshakes (for 5 people); and so on)* Students might also notice that the next number of handshakes equals the number of the previous number of handshakes plus the number of children in the previous group. Write 6, 7, and 8 in the left column, and ask students to use the pattern to help you fill in the right column *(15, 21, 28)*. When students have completed the table, say: **With 8 people, there are 28 handshakes.**

Length and Metric Units

EXTEND LANGUAGE/ACCESS CONTENT

Objective Estimate and measure length in metric units, and choose the most appropriate metric unit of length for an object or distance.

Materials Pencil

Vocabulary Centimeter, meter

ESL Strategies *Use before* **LEARN**

⏱ 5–10 MIN

Focus on Meaning ➤ Write "<u>meter</u>" and "<u>centimeter</u>" on the board. Hold up a pencil. **Which of these units would we use to measure the length of this pencil?** Point to the word *meter*. **Would we use a meter?** *(No)* **Why not?** *(It's too long.)* **About how long is a meter?** *(Sample answers: A little more than a yard; about 3 feet)* Point to the word *centimeter*. **Would we use a centimeter?** *(Yes)* **Why?** *(It's smaller than the pencil.)* **About how long is a centimeter?** *(Sample answers: $\frac{1}{100}$ of a meter; less than half an inch)*

Use Graphic Organizers ➤ Draw two word webs on the board. Start with two center ovals, one labeled "Centimeter" and the other labeled "Meter." Help students brainstorm lengths (or widths or heights) of objects or distances that are about each of the units. As words and lengths are called out, write them in the surrounding ovals of the web. As an alternative to having students call out words and phrases, have volunteers come to the board one at a time to write their suggestions directly in the web.

Capacity and Metric Units

ACCESS CONTENT

Objective Estimate and measure capacity in milliliters and liters, and choose the most appropriate metric unit for the capacity of a container.

Materials Pictures of containers varying in size; *(per pair)* paper or poster board; scissors; paste (or glue)

Vocabulary Liter, milliliter

ESL Strategies *Use before* **LEARN**

⏱ 15 MIN

Use Pictures ➤ Hold up a picture of a cup. **This is a container. What do we use containers for?** *(To hold things)* **We can fill it with soup. The amount this container can hold is called its capacity. Would we use milliliters or liters to measure the capacity of this bowl?** *(Milliliters)* **Hold up a picture of a bathtub. This is another container. We can fill it with water. Would we use milliliters or liters to measure the capacity of this bathtub?** *(Liters)*

Have students pair up, and distribute 4 four pictures of containers to each pair. Have students talk to their partners about the most appropriate unit to use in measuring the capacity of each container. Then ask each pair to record their choices by making a poster. Have students use the headings "Milliliters" and "Liters" and paste their pictures under the appropriate heading. Invite students to explain their choices for the completed poster to the class.

Mass and Metric Units

USE WITH LESSON
11-11

ACCESS CONTENT

Objective Estimate and measure mass in grams and kilograms, and choose the most appropriate metric unit of mass for an object.

Materials *(per group)* Gram weight, kilogram weight

Vocabulary Mass, gram, kilogram

ESL Strategies   *Use before* **CHECK** ✓   ⏱ 5–10 MIN

Use Real Objects ➤   Write the words "<u>gram</u>" and "<u>kilogram</u>" on the board. Say the words aloud, and have students repeat them after you. Then divide the class into groups and give each group a gram weight and a kilogram weight. Tell students to take turns holding both the weights to get an idea of how they compare. **Which is lighter?** *(The gram weight)* **Which is heavier?** *(The kilogram weight)* **We can use grams to measure the mass of light objects. We can use kilograms to measure the mass of heavy objects. What do you think** *mass* **means?** *(Weight)*

Use Small-Group ➤
Interactions
  Have groups of students play a guessing game. Model how to play with one group. One student makes a statement such as, "I'm thinking of something that has a mass of a few grams. You write with it." The remaining group members guess names of objects that might fit the description. The person who names the correct object (in this case, a pencil) describes another object with a mass of either a few grams or a few kilograms. Play continues until each student has made one descriptive statement.

Changing Units and Comparing Measures

ACCESS CONTENT

Objective Change units of length, capacity, and mass to equivalent units and compare measures.

ESL Strategies | *Use before* **CHECK ✓**   ⏱ 5–10 MIN

Use ➤
Demonstration

Write the following equations on the board and read them aloud.

> 2 meters = _____ centimeters
>
> 3 liters = _____ milliliters
>
> 5 kilograms = _____ grams

Which unit is larger, a meter or a centimeter? *(Meter)* **Which unit is larger, a liter or a milliliter?** *(Liter)* **Which unit is larger, a kilogram or a gram?** *(Kilogram)*

Write the following sentence on the board and read it aloud. "To change larger units to smaller units, multiply." Have students repeat the statement in unison. Then complete each conversion. After each, have a volunteer come to the board to write the multiplication sentence needed to solve each conversion. *(2 × 100 = 200 centimeters; 3 × 1,000 = 3,000 milliliters; 5 × 1,000 = 5,000 grams)*

Repeat the activity with the following examples. Ask students to identify the smaller unit in each equation before you begin.

> 400 centimeters = _____ meters
>
> 8,000 milliliters = _____ liters
>
> 3,000 grams = _____ kilograms

Write the following on the board, and have students repeat it in unison: "To change from smaller units to larger units, divide." Then have a volunteer come to the board to complete each conversion by writing a division sentence. *(400 centimeters ÷ 100 = 4 meters; 8,000 milliliters ÷ 1,000 = 8 liters; 3,000 grams ÷ 1,000 = 3 kilograms)*

Problem-Solving Skill: Writing to Explain

EXTEND LANGUAGE

USE WITH LESSON 11-13

Objective Write to explain a prediction.

ESL Strategies

Use before LEARN

⏱ 10 MIN

> **Have Students Report Back in Writing**

Write the following data statements on the board, and then read them aloud.

> Nadia played 4 games of basketball. In the first game, she scored 21 points. In the second game, she scored 20 points. In the third game, she scored 23 points, and in the fourth game, she scored 19 points.

Do you think Nadia will score more than 40 points in the next game she plays? *(No)* **Why not?** *(She scored about 20 points in each of the first 4 games she played.)* **How many points do you think Nadia will score in the next game she plays?** *(About 20 points)*

Have pairs of students work together to write at least three sets of related data statements (at least 3) that can be used to make a prediction. Invite students to refer to the data statements on the board to use as a model, but remind them that they should use different information. When students have finished, have pairs exchange their data statements with another pair. Each group of students then writes a prediction based on the data. Then the two pairs get together to discuss whether or not the predictions are reasonable or close to what was expected.

Temperature

EXTEND LANGUAGE

USE WITH LESSON 11-14

Objective Read temperatures above and below zero on Fahrenheit and Celsius thermometers, and determine appropriate temperatures for given activities.

Materials Fahrenheit and Celsius thermometer; (per student) picture of Fahrenheit and Celsius thermometer,; red and blue crayons

Vocabulary Degrees Fahrenheit (°F), degrees Celsius (°C)

ESL Strategies

Use before CHECK ✓

⏱ 5–10 MIN

> **Focus on Meaning**

Display the thermometer. **We use a thermometer to find temperature, What does temperature tell us?** *(How hot or how cold something is.)* Write 68°F and 18°C on the board. **We can measure temperature in** <u>degrees Fahrenheit</u> **or** <u>degrees Celsius</u>. Point to the degree symbol in each temperature. **We write the symbol for degrees like this.**

Give each student a red and a blue crayon and a picture of a thermometer. Explain that the thermometer is marked with scales for both degrees Fahrenheit (on the right) and degrees Celsius (on the left). **On the Celsius scale, water boils at 100°C.** Have students draw a red line at the 100 mark. **Water freezes at 0°C.** Have students draw a blue line at the 0 mark. **At what temperature does water boil on the Fahrenheit scale? Look at the temperature across 100°C.** *(212°F)* **At what temperature does water and freezes on the Fahrenheit scale?** *(32°F)* Help students see that the lines they drew mark the same two levels on the thermometer. Then discuss with students what the temperature in both scales might be on a hot day *(Sample answer: 95°F or 35°C)* and on a cold day *(Sample answer: 40°F or 5°C)*.

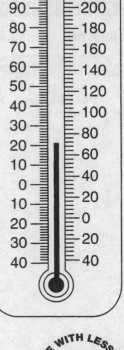

Problem-Solving Applications: Woodlands

USE WITH LESSON
11-15

ACCESS CONTENT

Objective Review and apply key concepts, skills, and strategies learned in this and previous chapters.

ESL Strategies

Use Small-Group Interactions

Use before CHECK ✓

⏱ 5–10 MIN

Write the following word problem on the board, excluding the answer, and then read it aloud.

> Carlos collects stamps. About $\frac{1}{4}$ of his stamps are from Mexico. What fraction of Carlos's stamps are not from Mexico? $(\frac{3}{4})$

Have students work in pairs to solve the problem. When all groups are finished, have one pair of students explain meet with another pair to talk about their strategy for solving the problem to another pair. Then the second pair explains their solution strategy. Suggest that pairs discuss similarities and differences among strategies.

Inequalities on a Number Line

ACTIVATE PRIOR KNOWLEDGE/BUILD BACKGROUND

Objective Solve an inequality by graphing the inequality on a number line.

Materials Linear measuring devices with customary units
(for example: inch ruler, yardstick, customary tape measure)

ESL Strategies

Connect to Prior Knowledge of Math

Use before **LEARN**   🕐 10–15 MIN

Show a variety of linear measuring devices, such as an inch ruler, a yardstick, and a customary tape measure. Point to each and say the name aloud for students to repeat. Hold each one up, one at a time, and ask students to name things (for example, a candy bar, a door frame, a carpet) they could measure with each device. *(Sample answers: Candy bar, door frame, carpet)* **These measuring tools are examples of number lines. They all show numbers marked in order.**

Draw a number line on the board as shown below. Point to it as you say: **This number line shows 0 and the whole numbers 1 through 10.** Point to the letter A and to the number 5 on the number line as you say: **All the numbers to the left of A are less than 5. Which numbers are less than 5?** *(0, 1, 2, 3, and 4)* **All the numbers to the right of A are greater than 5. Which numbers are greater than 5?** *(6, 7, 8, 9, and 10)*

Have students come to the board and label other whole numbers on the number line with capital letters. Then have them identify by pointing out to the class numbers that are less than and greater than the labeled number that you call out. Encourage students to respond in complete sentences such as, "The numbers ____, ____, and ____ are greater than ____; the numbers ____, ____, and ____, are less than ____."

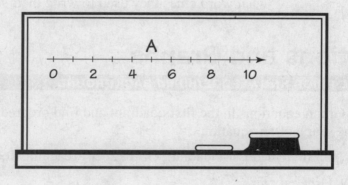

Translating Words to Equations

EXTEND LANGUAGE

Objective Write equations for word sentences.

Materials *(per group)* Index card labeled $+$, $-$, $\times$, and $\div$

Vocabulary Equation

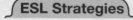

Use before **CHECK** ✓   ⏱ 10 MIN

Focus on Meaning ➤ **You have learned that when you solve word problems, you often need to write a number sentence. What is this number sentence called?** *(An equation)* **When you read the problem, you look for words that tell which operation to use. What words are clues that you need to use addition?** *(Sample answers: Plus, more, altogether)* Take several responses from students, and write them on the board. Do the same for subtraction, multiplication, and division. Then write the following sentence on the board.

Five pencils and some more pencils are eleven pencils altogether.

What clues in this sentence tells us which operation to use? *(And, more)* Demonstrate writing the equation "$5 + x = 11$" beneath the sentence. As you write each part, ask students to identify the correspondences, which words in the problem correspond to the numbers and symbols in the equation. For example: 5 for *five pencils*, $+$ for *and*, x for *some more*, $=$ for *are* and 11 for *eleven pencils*. Align each part of the equation with the corresponding word above it.

Assign students to groups. Give each group an index card with a different operation symbol on it. Have each group write three different sentences that involve the operation on their card. If possible, assign at least one student who is proficient in English to each group. Then have each groups exchange sentences with another group, and writing equations for the other groups' one another's sentences. Ask one member of each group to report to the class what word clues they used to write their sentences and equations

Equations and Graphs

ACTIVATE PRIOR KNOWLEDGE/BUILD BACKGROUND

Objective Graph equations in the first quadrant and find ordered pairs on the graph of an equation.

Materials *(per student)* First-Quadrant Grid Paper (Teaching Tool 18)

Vocabulary Ordered pair

Use before **LEARN** 🕐 5 MIN

Connect to Prior ➤ Knowledge of Math

Write the following <u>ordered pairs</u> on the board.

(9, 7)   (7, 5)   (5, 3)   (4, 2)   (2, 0)

Draw or display a grid on the board. **You have used ordered pairs before to show points on a grid.** Point to the first ordered pair. **What does the first number in an ordered pair tell you?** *(The number of spaces to move to the right)* **What does the second number in an ordered pair tell you?** *(The number of spaces to move up)* **How do I locate this point?** *(Move 9 spaces to the right 9, then move up 7 spaces.)* Have a volunteer come to the grid and mark the point for the first ordered pair as others mark their own grids. Repeat the procedure until all points have been plotted. **What do you notice about these points?** *(They are all in a straight line.)*

Point to the ordered pairs. **We can show these ordered pairs a different way.** On the board, draw the function table shown in the illustration below. Make sure students realize that each row of the chart is identical to one of the ordered pairs. **What rule tells you how to find the number in the y column?** *(Subtract 2)* **We call this the value for y. So, to find the y value in each pair, we subtract 2 from the x value for x. What number sentence can we write to show this?** *(y = x − 2)* Write "y = x − 2" on the board. Then, on the grid, connect all the points. **We call this line a graph. This graph that shows solutions to the equation y = x − 2.** Have several students pick points on the line and test them to see if they satisfy the equation.

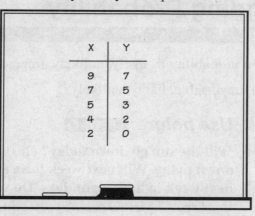

Problem-Solving Skill:
Extra or Missing Information

USE WITH LESSON

12-4

ACCESS CONTENT

Objective Solve problems involving too much information by using only the information needed, and decide when there is not enough information to solve a problem.

Use before **LEARN** 🕐 10–15 MIN

Use ➤ Demonstration

Write the following problem on the board. Invite students to read aloud the problem with you.

Every week, Anna puts some of her allowance into her bank account. How much more money did she put in this week than last week?

Does this problem give you enough information to answer the question? *(No)* Ask a student to tell you what additional information is needed to solve the problem. *(How much money Anna put into her account this week and how much she put in last week)*

Change the problem on the board to read as follows. Invite students to read aloud the problem with you.

Every week, Anna puts some of her allowance into her bank account. She has $234 in her account. Last week she put $6 in the bank. This week she put $8 in the bank. How much more money did she put in this week than last week?

Can you solve the problem now? *(Yes)* **What do you need to do?** *(Subtract the amount of money Anna put in the bank last week from the amount of money she put in the bank this week.)* **What is the solution?** *($8 − $6 = $2)* **Is there any information that you don't need in order to solve it?** *(Yes)* **What is the extra information?** *(The total amount of money in her bank account)*

Use Small-Group Interactions ➤ Have pairs of students write simple problems with missing or extra information. Then have volunteers read their problems aloud to the class and have the class identify if there is missing or extra information in it.

Understanding Probability

EXTEND LANGUAGE

USE WITH LESSON 12-5

Objective Describe a probability as likely, unlikely, impossible, or certain.

Vocabulary Certain, impossible, likely, unlikely

ESL Strategies

Use before **CHECK** ✓   🕐 10 MIN

Use Simulation ➤ **Will the sun go down today?** *(Yes)* **So it is <u>certain</u> that the sun will go down today. Will next week have eight days?** *(No)* **So it is <u>impossible</u> for next week to have eight days. Do you think you will have breakfast tomorrow?** *(Answers may vary.)* **So you will probably have breakfast tomorrow. It is <u>likely</u> that you will. Do you think you will ride a horse to school tomorrow?** *(No)* **So it is <u>unlikely</u> that you will.** Write the following statements on the board and have students read them in unison.

If something <u>must</u> happen, it is <u>certain</u>.
If something <u>cannot</u> happen, it is <u>impossible</u>.
If something <u>will probably</u> happen, it is <u>likely</u> that it will happen.
If something <u>will probably not</u> happen, it is <u>unlikely</u> that it will happen.

Which word tells whether you will wear shoes to school tomorrow? *(Likely)* **Which word tells whether you will grow to be twenty feet tall?** *(Impossible)* **Which word tells whether school will end today?** *(Certain)* **Which word tells when something cannot happen?** *(Impossible)* **Which word tells when something will probably happen?** *(Likely)* **Which word tells whether it will snow tomorrow when something will probably not happen?** *(Unlikely)*

Listing Outcomes

ACTIVATE PRIOR KNOWLEDGE/BUILD BACKGROUND

Objective List all possible results for a situation.

Materials *(per group of 5)* Brown paper bag,; set of 54 cards colored with dots: 21 red, 1 yellow, 1 green, 1 blue

Vocabulary Outcome

ESL Strategies

Use Simulation ➤

Use before **LEARN**   🕙 10–15 MIN

Divide the class into groups of 4. Give each group a bag containing colored cards. Have each student pick a card from the bag without looking. Then have them record the color of their card and return it to the bag. Once each group member has picked a card say: **Raise your hands if you picked a green card. Repeat the instruction for other color cards—red, yellow, and blue.** Record the results on the board. Have the groups empty their bags and look at their cards.

What 4 cards could you have picked from the bag? As the students respond, write the list on the board. *(Red, yellow, green, blue)* **These possible results of picking a card from the bag are called** <u>outcomes</u>. **These 4 results — two red cards, the yellow card, the green card, and the blue card — are the possible outcomes. It is possible that you will pick any one of these 4 cards from the bag. Suppose I take away the blue card from your bag. Now what are the possible outcomes?** *(Red, yellow, green)* **Could purple be an outcome?** *(No)* **Why not?** *(Because there are no purple cards in the bag; it is impossible to pick a purple card.)*

Finding Probability

ACCESS CONTENT; EXTEND LANGUAGE

Objective Use a fraction to express the probability of an event.

Materials Crayons: 5 blue, 3 red, 2 yellow; 3 marbles of different colors; paper bag; spinner with each of 4 sections a different color; cube with sides of different colors; set of 10 cards, with dots of 5 different colors (2 cards per color)

ESL Strategies   *Use before* **LEARN**   🕐 15 MIN

Use ➤
Demonstration

When we talk about the probability that something might happen, we are talking about how likely it is that the event will happen. If there are dark clouds in the sky, how likely is it that it will rain? *(Sample answers: Fairly likely, very likely)*

Sometimes we can be more specific about the probability of something happening. Display the crayons and the paper bag (see Materials). **Count the crayons of each color that I am putting into this bag.** Have students count with you as you put the crayons in the bag and record the number of each color. **We're going to find the probability of picking a red crayon from the bag. How many crayons in all are in the bag?** *(10)* **How many of them are red?** *(3)* **So 3 out of the 10 crayons are red.** Write "3 out of 10" on the board. **What fraction can we write to show 3 parts of a set of 10?** $(\frac{3}{10})$ **So the probability of picking a red crayon is 3 out of 10, or $\frac{3}{10}$.** Repeat with the yellow and blue crayons. *(Yellow: 2 out of 10 is $\frac{2}{10}$, or $\frac{1}{5}$; blue: 5 out of 10 is $\frac{5}{10}$, or $\frac{1}{2}$.)*

Have Students ➤
Report Back
Orally

Divide the class into 4 groups. Give 1 group the spinner, another group the marbles in the bag, the third group the cube, and the last group the set of cards (see Materials). In turns, ask each group to come to the front of the room and describe what you gave them. Then ask a probability-related question. For example: **What is the probability that the spinner will land on red?** *(1 out of 4, or $\frac{1}{4}$)* **What is the probability that green will come out on top when you toss the cube?** *(1 out of 6, or $\frac{1}{6}$)* Each time, have students explain the reasoning for their answers.

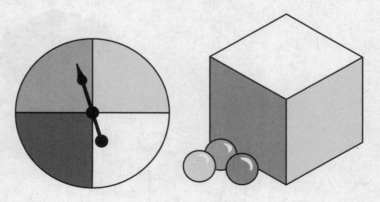

Making Predictions

ACCESS CONTENT

Objective Make predictions.

Materials *(per group)* Spinner with each of 4 sections a different color (Teaching Tool 20)

Vocabulary Prediction

ESL Strategies   *Use before*   **LEARN**   🕐 15 MIN

Use Small-Group Interactions ➤

Lead students in a discussion relating probability to making <u>predictions</u>. **If I toss a coin, what is the probability that it will land on the front side of the coin?** *($\frac{1}{2}$, or 1 out of 2)* **So if I toss a coin more than once, does that mean that it will land on the front side exactly half the time?** *(No)* **Why not?** *(Sample answer: A prediction is an estimate.)*

Divide the class into 4 groups. Give each group a spinner. Have students in each group take turns spinning the spinner until they record the results of 12 spins. On the board, write four headings: "Group 1," "Group 2," "Group 3," and "Group 4." To the left of the columns, write "12 spins." **What is the probability that the spinner will land on red?** *($\frac{1}{4}$, or 1 in 4)* **If I spin it 12 times, about how many times should it land on red?** *(About 3 times)* **How do you know?** *($12 \times \frac{1}{4} = 3$)* Write "about $\frac{3}{12}$" on the board. Have one student in each group tell the actual number of red outcomes for his or her group's 12 spins. Write the results in fraction form, $\frac{x}{12}$, on the board in the appropriate columns.

Have students record red outcomes for a second set of 12 spins. Then write "24 spins" to the left of the columns on the board. **If I spin a spinner 24 times, about how many times should the spinner land on red**? *(About 6 times)* How do you know? *($24 \times \frac{1}{4} = 6$)* Write "about $\frac{6}{24}$" on the board. Have a different student in each group tell the actual number of red outcomes for his or her group's second set of 12 spins. Add these numbers to the original outcomes in the appropriate columns, and write the results in fraction form *($\frac{x}{24}$)*. **Which number of spins had outcomes that were closer to the probability of spinning red?** *(Answers may vary, but 24 spins should have yielded a result closer to the theoretical probability.)*

Problem-Solving Strategy: Work Backward

ACCESS CONTENT

Objective Solve problems that require finding the original times, measurements, or quantities that led to a result that is given.

Materials *(per pair)* Clock face

Use before **CHECK** ☑   ⏱ 10 MIN

Use Manipulatives ➤ Write the following problem, excluding the answer, on the board, and then read it aloud.

> The time is now 4:10 P.M. Ramon has been mowing the lawn for 15 minutes. At what time did Ramon start mowing the lawn? (3:55 P.M.)

Have pairs of students use their clock faces to solve the problem. Ask one student from each pair to explain how they used the Work Backward strategy to solve the problem.

Problem-Solving Applications: Fire-Fighting Helicopters

ACTIVATE PRIOR KNOWLEDGE/BUILD BACKGROUND

Objective Review and apply key concepts, skills, and strategies learned in this and previous chapters.

Materials *(per group)* Bill and Coin Models (Teaching Tool 7)

Vocabulary Text

Use before **LEARN**   ⏱ 5 MIN

Use Role Playing ➤ Write the following word problem on the board, excluding the answer, and then read it aloud.

> Mia has $15.75. Juan has twice as much money as Mia. How much money does Juan have? ($31.50)

Have pairs of students use the coins and bills to act out the problem. One student models the amount of money Mia has, and the other student adds to those bills and coins to model the amount of money Juan has, exchanging for dollar bills and other coin types as necessary. When all groups are finished, have pairs of students compare their strategies for using the bill and coin models to solve the problem.